GUIDELINES

VOL 31 / PART 3
September–December 2015

Commissioned by **David Sprig**

Guidelines © BRF 2015

The Bible Reading Fellowship
15 The Chambers, Vineyard, Abingdon OX14 3FE
Tel: 01865 319700; Fax: 01865 319701
E-mail: enquiries@brf.org.uk; Websites: www.brf.org.uk; www.biblereadingnotes.org.uk

ISBN 978 0 85746 134 6

Distributed in Australia by Mediacom Education Inc., PO Box 610, Unley, SA 5061.
Tel: 1800 811 311; Fax: 08 8297 8719;
E-mail: admin@mediacom.org.au
Available also from all good Christian bookshops in Australia.
For individual and group subscriptions in Australia:
Mrs Rosemary Morrall, PO Box W35, Wanniassa, ACT 2903.

Distributed in New Zealand by Scripture Union Wholesale, PO Box 760, Wellington
Tel: 04 385 0421; Fax: 04 384 3990; E-mail: suwholesale@clear.net.nz

Publications distributed to more than 60 countries

Acknowledgments

The New Revised Standard Version of the Bible, Anglicised Edition, copyright © 1989, 1995 by the Division of Christian Education of the National Council of the Churches of Christ in the USA. Used by permission. All rights reserved.

The Holy Bible, New International Version (Anglicised Edition), copyright © 1979, 1984, 2011 by Biblica. Used by permission of Hodder & Stoughton Publishers, an Hachette UK company. All rights reserved. 'NIV' is a registered trademark of Biblica. UK trademark number 1448790.

The New American Standard Bible®, Copyright © 1960, 1962, 1963, 1968, 1971, 1972, 1973, 1975, 1977, 1995 by The Lockman Foundation. Used by permission. (www.Lockman.org)

Extracts from The Book of Common Prayer of 1662, the rights of which are vested in the Crown in perpetuity within the United Kingdom, are reproduced by permission of Cambridge University Press, Her Majesty's Printers.

Printed by Gutenberg Press, Tarxien, Malta.

Suggestions for using *Guidelines*

Set aside a regular time and place, if possible, when you can read and pray undisturbed. Before you begin, take time to be still and, if you find it helpful, use the BRF prayer.

In *Guidelines*, the introductory section provides context for the passages or themes to be studied, while the units of comment can be used daily, weekly, or whatever best fits your timetable. You will need a Bible (more than one if you want to compare different translations) as Bible passages are not included. At the end of each week is a 'Guidelines' section, offering further thoughts about, or practical application of what you have been studying.

Occasionally, you may read something in *Guidelines* that you find particularly challenging, even uncomfortable. This is inevitable in a series of notes which draws on a wide spectrum of contributors, and doesn't believe in ducking difficult issues. Indeed, we believe that *Guidelines* readers much prefer thought-provoking material to a bland diet that only confirms what they already think.

If you do disagree with a contributor, you may find it helpful to go through these three steps. First, think about why you feel uncomfortable. Perhaps this is an idea that is new to you, or you are not happy at the way something has been expressed. Or there may be something more substantial—you may feel that the writer is guilty of sweeping generalisation, factual error, theological or ethical misjudgment. Second, pray that God would use this disagreement to teach you more about his word and about yourself. Third, think about what you will do as a result of the disagreement. You might resolve to find out more about the issue, or write to the contributor or the editors of *Guidelines*.

To send feedback, you may email or write to BRF at the addresses shown opposite. If you would like your comment to be included on our website, please email connect@brf.org.uk. You can also Tweet to @brfonline, using the hashtag #brfconnect.

Writers in this issue

Brian Howell has lectured in Old Testament at several universities and institutions around the UK, and is currently the Dean of Studies and Research at Bible Society. He is also a jazz saxophonist and professional kid wrestler (but only against the fearsome tag team of Jayden and Jazmine).

Paula Gooder is Theologian in Residence for the Bible Society. Her specialism is St Paul, particularly 2 Corinthians, but she has a strong and abiding love for the Gospels—especially the Gospel of Mark. She lives in Birmingham with her husband and two daughters.

Oldi Morava is currently working with Bible Society to translate the Old Testament into Albanian as part of an interconfessional team. He graduated from Redcliffe College with a BA in Applied Theology and later completed a Masters in Biblical Hebrew at Oxford University. He is married with one daughter.

Steve Walton is a researcher and teacher in New Testament and an Anglican priest. He is Professorial Research Fellow at St Mary's University, Twickenham, and Honorary Research Fellow at Tyndale House, Cambridge. Steve is presently working on a major commentary on Acts.

Alec Gilmore, a Baptist minister and a frequent contributor to *Guidelines*. has contributed to many Christian publications in the UK and US and written extensively on Baptist and ecumenical affairs as well as biblical studies. His most recent book is *A Concise Dictionary of Bible Origins and Interpretation* (T&T Clark/Continuum).

Andrew Lincoln is Emeritus Professor of New Testament at the University of Gloucestershire. His publications include substantial commentaries on Ephesians, Colossians and the Gospel of John.

Stephen Holmes is Senior Lecturer in Systematic Theology at the University of St Andrews and offers theological consultancy to Christian organisations engaged in public policy work. He chairs the Theology and Public Policy Advisory Commission for the Evangelical Alliance.

David Spriggs has retired from Bible Society but continues his work with them as a consultant. His main role is as a team minister at the Hinckley Baptist Church, where he has special responsibility to work with the leaders.

David Spriggs writes...

From Joseph to Jesus—that is the spread covered by our readings in this issue as we head towards Advent and Christmas. We begin with Brian Howell elucidating for us the great narrative of Joseph in Genesis 37—50. This is an amazing story of divine promises, human suffering and enduring trust in God's faithfulness, and of God's provision to save not only his own people (in the form of Joseph's family) but also the 'arch enemy', the Egyptians, from a devastating famine.

Under Paula Gooder's expert tuition, we spend three weeks travelling with Jesus towards the cross. Mark's telling of the gospel story is marked by controversy, conflict and foreboding. This too is a story of divine promises, human suffering and enduring trust in God's faithfulness, through which God provides for our salvation.

Oldi Morava shares his insights with us as we explore another pivotal time in Israel's history, as the nation moves towards monarchy and becomes aware of the pitfalls that go with it. The struggles of King Saul are illuminated by the promises of God to David and David's friendship with Jonathan.

Continuing the travel theme, Steve Walton leads us through the second half of the book of Acts, from Athens to Rome. Paul arrives there, a prisoner, to bear witness to his faith at the heart of the empire.

All the more reason for exploring the letter that Paul wrote in preparation for his visit! Andrew Lincoln shares his deep lifelong learning about Paul as he takes us through the letter to the Romans. These three weeks' notes are not to be missed, and, rather like the chapters from Mark's Gospel, take us into both the heart of darkness and the heart of God.

Between Acts and Romans, we are delighted to welcome back Alec Gilmore, who writes on Malachi. Alec's passion to help us engage with the significance of this ancient text for our own lives ensures that we meet some profound challenges. Here is one sentence to whet your appetites! 'This community appears to have lost its roots, and has broken not only the relationship but the heart of God into the bargain.'

With Advent well under way, Steve Holmes helps us explore the riches of the doctrine of incarnation, by looking at scriptures that 'prefigure', 'explain' and 'presume' it. His second week explores the full humanity of Jesus. In between, for Christmas week itself, I offer some reflections on the first two chapters of Luke's Gospel.

The BRF Prayer

Almighty God,
you have taught us that your word is a lamp for our
feet and a light for our path. Help us, and all who
prayerfully read your word, to deepen our
fellowship with you and with each other through your love.
And in so doing may we come to know you more fully,
love you more truly, and follow more faithfully in
the steps of your son Jesus Christ, who lives and
reigns with you and the Holy Spirit,
one God for evermore. Amen.

A Prayer for Remembrance

Heavenly Father, we commit ourselves to work in
penitence and faith for reconciliation between the
nations, that all people may, together, live in
freedom, justice and peace. We pray for all who
in bereavement, disability and pain continue to
suffer the consequences of fighting and terror.
We remember with thanksgiving and sorrow those
whose lives, in world wars and conflicts past and
present, have been given and taken away.

FROM AN ORDER OF SERVICE FOR REMEMBRANCE SUNDAY,
CHURCHES TOGETHER IN BRITAIN AND IRELAND 2005

Genesis 37—50

Genesis is divided into three sections: the proto-history (chs. 1—11), the Abraham cycle (chs. 12—36) and the so-called Joseph cycle (chs. 37—50). These sections can be seen as setting up the original problem of humanity, the promise of a cure, and its initial outworking. God's promises to Abraham begin to take shape in the growth of his clan and in Joseph's own reputation and blessing to the world.

Although Genesis 37—50 is often known as the 'Joseph cycle', the narrative is actually called the history of Jacob (37:2). It is interested in all of Jacob's sons, as seen in his blessing of each of them in chapter 49. Notably, the lead characters are those whose names are explained with reference to Yahweh: Reuben, Simeon, Judah and Joseph (29:32, 33, 35; 30:24). The rift between Jacob and his sons occurs in chapters 34—35, while that between the brothers themselves is found in chapter 37. The story of the schism, how it is mended, and the ensuing development of the brothers' characters provide the structure for this last part of Genesis.

One element of this structure involves the tension between the sons and their father. When Reuben sleeps with Jacob's concubine Bilhah (after Rachel's death), he is probably seeking not only to usurp his father's authority (see Genesis 9:22–27; 19:33–38; 2 Samuel 3:7–8; 16:21–22) but also to prevent Rachel's maid from becoming the new favourite wife, ahead of his own mother, Leah, who was unloved (Genesis 29:31; see Wenham, *Genesis 16—50*, p. 327). The contempt he shows his father may derive from Jacob's inaction on hearing of the rape of Reuben's (full) sister, Dinah. This sets up tension between the sons of Leah and the sons of Rachel (along with those of their respective maids), as well as with their ominously unresponsive father. These issues will be in the background of the rest of chapters 37—50.

Another aspect of the background is the relationship between the sons. History repeats itself in both Jacob's and Joseph's lives as their fathers show favouritism to one son, leading to poor behaviour on the favoured son's part, followed by a destructive response from the unfavoured. Joseph's handling of his favour and his dreams presents a dramatic background not only to the development of his own faith but also to the question of how God interacts with human choices.

Biblical quotations are taken from the New American Standard Bible.

1 Joseph's dreams and sale

Genesis 37

After Jacob's return to Canaan, we see the break-up of his family. His brother Esau, though reconciled, goes his separate way (36:6). His first-born sleeps with his concubine (35:22) and his next two sons commit a slaughter (34:25). He turns his attention to the son of his favoured wife, Rachel, but Joseph plays his own role in the deterioration of the family, starting by giving a 'bad report' of his brothers (v. 2). Although we are not aware of the content of the report, the Hebrew term *dbh* ('to give a report') is always used in a negative sense (Wenham, p. 350). Because the writer puts it like this, it serves to characterise Joseph as somewhat immature, like a tell-tale, rather than highlighting the brothers' naughtiness.

Next, Joseph has some dreams. Oddly, this first of the three pairs of dreams that Joseph interprets is the only one with no mention of God. This throws doubt not as much upon the provenance of the dreams (they did, after all, come true) as on Joseph's interpretation of them. Dreams were commonly viewed in the Ancient Near East as divine revelations, so they would represent a significant event in Joseph's life, but his readiness to share them with his family makes a bad situation worse. At best it demonstrates naivety on Joseph's part about the situation brewing with his brothers. At worst, it represents a sort of spiritual pride regarding God's speaking into his life. In any case, Joseph's unwise action results in the brothers 'adding' (v. 5) hate to Joseph (which means 'he adds')—one of several plays on Joseph's name. The brothers' response (v. 8) is akin to 'pulling rank', as they ask who this younger brother is who will rule over them (Wenham, p. 352).

Despite Reuben's innocent cries, the brothers callously continue with their falsified report of Joseph's death, ironically using the same implements (goat kid and garment) that Jacob used to deceive his own father (27:15–16).

2 Judah and Tamar

Genesis 38

This episode seems like an interruption in the Joseph story, but there are some parallels that tie it to its context. Joseph's brothers command Jacob to 'examine' his torn and bloodied coat (37:32); likewise, Judah is told to 'examine' the staff and signet ring (38:25). In addition, a kid goat plays a part in both stories (37:31; 38:17). Thus, we are led to consider the relevance of this momentary focus on Judah.

Judah commands his second son, Onan, to perform a 'levirate' marriage (from the Latin *levir*, meaning 'brother-in-law'). The duties of the levirate were to raise up children for, and thus carry on the name of, his deceased brother (Deuteronomy 25:5–6). Onan refuses to do this, although we can only speculate on his reasons. As the firstborn's double share of the inheritance would have come to him next, he might have been refusing to create an heir who would take precedence over himself. However, his refusal is more odious than it might at first appear. The Hebrew indicates that the 'wasting of his seed' was a habitual act. Thus, for either using or cheating Tamar, he dies like his brother.

Judah fails to give his last son to the woman with whom his other two have died. Technically, she was betrothed to Shelah, which is why Judah demands that she be burned upon finding her pregnant (v. 24). The first readers of this story would have been aware that Old Testament law regarded sex with another man during the betrothal period as adultery, but the law would also have condemned both parties to death (Deuteronomy 22:13–21, 23–24). The death penalty in this case is ameliorated, probably due to Judah's unwittingness and the injustice done to Tamar.

The location of Tamar's ruse is the key to the episode. Enaim is, literally translated, the 'opening of the eyes' (Victor Hamilton, *The Book of Genesis Chapters 18—50*, p. 440). This is the place where Judah's eyes are opened (see Genesis 3:5, 7). In being deceived as he has deceived others, Judah comes to understand that Tamar is more righteous than he. He tried to preserve his son from an innocent woman who seemed cursed, but she carries on the line of a truly cursed man, at her own peril. Ultimately, the younger of Tamar's twins, Perez, will be an ancestor of King David (Ruth 4:18–22) and, ultimately, of Christ.

3 Potiphar's wife

Potiphar was a high official, possibly the captain of Pharaoh's bodyguard (v. 1; 37:36). However, the term used to describe him can mean 'chief of cooks', so he may have been head over Pharaoh's domestic affairs and catering, much like a butler. Despite the awful turn of events for Joseph, it is repeatedly underscored that God's presence is with him. Potiphar recognises it and attempts to make the most of it by setting Joseph over his house, perhaps in the same way that he himself was over Pharaoh's house. However, this sets up the potential for great jealousy between Joseph and the other servants (another prominent theme in Genesis 37—50), which will bring him down.

There is a subcurrent to this text—that of the relationship between Potiphar and his wife. She remains unnamed, which typically means that she is serving as an agent whose purpose is to further the plot or to be a foil, providing a contrast with some other character. Not only does she attempt to seduce Joseph, but she even blames her husband for bringing Joseph in, both to the servants and to his face (vv. 14, 17). We can suspect that there is something awry in the relationship within which Joseph finds himself caught.

Although Potiphar's wife's persistent lust for Joseph's figure is clearly behind the scandal, again we see Joseph foolishly playing into the hands of those who would undo him. Despite her daily advances, he is said to enter the house 'while there were no men of the household there' (v. 11). Like giving a bad report about his brothers and following it up by relating dreams of their subjugation to him, he once again acts innocently but foolishly. It is not enough simply to be free of guilt. We need also to be full of wisdom.

We are told that Potiphar is furious (v. 19), but the narrative does not tell us who is the target of his anger. It is striking that he does not simply have Joseph killed. Perhaps the prison sentence suggests an acknowledgement by Potiphar of Joseph's innocence; his fury may be directed at his wife, for both accosting, and costing Potiphar, the servant who quite clearly brought him blessing.

4 Pharaoh's dreams and their interpretation

Genesis 40—41

As the biblical writers tend to highlight only what is important to them, we may miss some of the feel of Joseph's ordeal. His stay with Potiphar and in prison actually totalled 13 years (37:2; 41:46), not just a few weeks or months. We are left to imagine the despair he must have struggled with in those times. Even in his darkest hours, however, God showed loyal love to him. It is clear that this did not mean shielding Joseph from all hurt or even from suffering the effects of his own foolishness. God did, however, go through Joseph's trials with him and gave him favour and hope within them (39:21).

Cupbearers' duties involved more than simply bringing and pouring the wine. They often became favourites of the king and occasionally wielded political influence (see Nehemiah 1:11). The baker in the prison was a chief baker, and, judging from ancient lists of Egyptian baked goods, his would have been quite a skilled position. The accusation against the two men was probably of treason, and this serves to build a strong contrast with the innocence of Joseph. Interestingly, it is possible that Potiphar was in charge of the royal prison, which seems to have been part of his own house (vv. 3–4). This could help to explain Joseph's strikingly similar promotion there, especially if Potiphar was, in fact, convinced of Joseph's innocence.

The consistent refrain in Joseph's dream interpretations polemically undercuts the common notion in the ancient Near East that dreams led the dreamer into the realm of heaven and the dead (Vergote, *Joseph en Égypte*, p. 48) but could be interpreted only by skilled specialists. Rather, Joseph insists that God is both the giver and the interpreter of dreams (40:8; 41:16, 25, 28). He interprets the repetition in Pharaoh's dreams as a sign that their fulfilment is both dependable and imminent (41:32). This is somewhat ironic, given that his own dreams included repetition (sun, moon and stars, *and* sheaves of wheat, all bowing to Joseph, in 37:7, 9) and yet it was nearly 30 years before they were fulfilled. God's notion of an impending fulfilment may not be as prompt as ours, but Joseph's life seems to argue that it is none the less certain.

5 An Egyptian connection

Genesis 42

Having followed Joseph's journeys, we now flash back to Canaan. The ten brothers are notably characterised in terms of their relationship with Joseph, ominously excluding Benjamin (vv. 3–4). Again, Jacob favours the other son of the wife he loved, refusing to send him to Egypt for food, afraid that 'harm may befall him' (v. 4). This not only shows his disregard for the harm that might befall the other ten, but perhaps indicates some lingering distrust about what they might do to this other son of Rachel.

Upon arriving in Egypt, the brothers quite explicitly fulfil Joseph's dream in bowing down to him. However, he knows that there is another brother, for eleven stars bowed down in his boyhood dream beside his mother and father (37:9). Joseph takes Simeon as collateral, either because he has now heard that Reuben did not participate in his sale into slavery (v. 22) or because he wants to hold Leah's second son in order to attain his mother Rachel's second son, Benjamin. However, the Joseph we find here is not the naive boy of even his time with Potiphar. He has grown wise and is playing a game on at least a couple of levels. He needs to discern whether or not his brothers' hearts have changed in the last 20 years. The testing he puts them through will either reveal the change or, perhaps, act as a catalyst to bring it about. In any case, reconciliation is not possible without a change of heart.

There is some irony in the brothers' response to Joseph's test. They have not been 'honest' men, as they claim (v. 31). This theme persists through the next part of the narrative, pressing the question: will they turn out to be honest men? Joseph's returning of their payment was done in secret, so they look like dishonest men (v. 25). They now feel that they will be accused of something falsely—much as Joseph himself was.

Only in verse 21 do we get a full picture of what happened between them when Joseph was thrown into the pit and then sold. It serves to highlight the brothers' come-uppance, but it is also ironic that they are recalling the scene now, as they haven't yet recognised Joseph. It seems that God is working in the brothers to confront them with their guilt.

6 Jacob's release

Genesis 43

So resolute is Jacob in his determination not to send Benjamin to Egypt that the family ends up eating all the grain, while leaving Simeon bound in Egypt (v. 2). Judah finally speaks up and takes personal responsibility for Benjamin's safety (v. 9), but he and his brothers are still trapped by their past and cannot tell their father the truth about Joseph.

Judah contrasts sharply with Reuben, a man who mishandled his frustration with his father's favouritism, and, ever since, has tried to make up for it, initially by saving Joseph from being killed. In Egypt, he piped up with an 'I told you so' (42:22), claiming that he, not Joseph, was the one to whom the brothers didn't listen. Then, back home, he offered his own two sons as collateral (42:37)—but it was not enough to erase what he had done.

Finally, Jacob resigns himself to God's hand and releases the last vestige of his beloved Rachel (vv. 13–14). When we throw ourselves upon God, it means being ready to face the worst possible consequence. It means submitting not just to his power to protect or bless, but to his sovereign choice in how to handle a matter. This recalls the episode at the Jabbok river, where Jacob finally sought not what he could cleverly con, but whatever God alone deigned to give (32:26). However, in reconciling with Esau, the brother he had duped, he still sent a large gift (32:13–21). Outward signs are needed to demonstrate inward change, especially when others may not have experienced the same change of heart.

When the brothers arrive in Egypt again, they are served separately from Joseph and his servants, the reason being that the Egyptians considered it disgusting to eat with Hebrews (v. 32). An early Aramaic translation of the text, *Targum Onkelos*, explains that this was because the Hebrews ate the cattle that the Egyptians worshipped. Although we cannot be sure of the exact reasons for it, this separation is a well-attested practice in Egypt, and its inclusion here testifies to the knowledge of the writer of Genesis.

Benjamin is given five times as much food as his brothers (v. 34). These extra portions would not necessarily have been consumed. They were a sign of favour—shown not because he was a full brother to Joseph, but because he was innocent of the harm done by his other siblings.

Guidelines

The story of Jacob's sons contains many themes, including wisdom, favouritism, pride, forgiveness and favour. We see Joseph being gifted by God and his father and handling both gifts poorly. In wearing his special tunic to meet his brothers, he flaunts the privilege he enjoys with his father over them. This compounds the problems of his tale-telling and inflames an already tense situation involving the sons of an unloved mother. Furthermore, he abuses the gift of the dreams he is given. Instead of passing the credit on to God, he uses it to make yet another jab at his brothers.

It is interesting that although Joseph did 'rule' over his brothers in Egypt, it was not from his line that the kings of Israel would eventually come. His vision, then, was not of a permanent hierarchy among the brothers, but only of his specific role in their deliverance from the famine. This might give us pause to ask how we have used the various gifts or words that God has given us. Have we used them to promote hope for others or to establish our own sense of worth as being more spiritually attuned than someone else?

Judah allows a paranoia to develop concerning Tamar, due to her association with his first two sons' deaths, and this leads him to defraud her. What stereotypes, biases or unwarranted associations have we allowed to colour the way we see and treat others?

Joseph was gifted with wisdom but he did not always make use of it, as is clear in the episode with Potiphar's wife. What situations have we allowed ourselves to get into that could cause our reputation or the reputation of Christ to be smeared? Even if we don't feel tempted to sin personally, what 'appearances' of evil are we allowing to flourish?

Finally, how can we follow Joseph's more promising characteristics in seeking God's favour within our circumstances rather than an escape from them?

1 The rise of Judah

Genesis 44

In this pivotal chapter, we finally see the cream rise to the top. Trouble has plagued Jacob's sons, in large part due to the favouritism he displayed with his wives and their respective sons. To recap, his firstborn has slept with his concubine, and his second and third sons have turned to brutality in revenge for their sister's rape. His fourth, Judah, has also been heading toward destruction. He married a Canaanite, in stark contrast with his great-grandfather Abraham (38:2; see 24:3–4). Although he prevented Joseph's death (37:26–27), Judah was complicit in his sale. He robbed his daughter-in-law of a husband. Finally, due to Tamar's bold initiative, he began to see the error of his ways. However, it is not until this present episode that Judah begins to take responsibility not only for himself but for his entire family. As he does so, we get a glimpse of the foundational character that will lead Judah to be the father of the royal tribe.

Joseph is still unsure about his brothers' real attitude to him: are they still jealous and hateful? To find out, he recreates the situation of his own sale into slavery. By tricking the brothers and making Benjamin look like a thief, he will force them to decide whether or not to return home without their younger brother, just as they had done with Joseph years before.

The parallels are not lost on the brothers. Although they still fail to recognise him, they are convinced that these harsh demands are justice for what they did to Joseph years earlier. The brothers respond not only in the solidarity of their grief but also in kindness to Benjamin, the son of Jacob's favoured wife.

Judah goes a step further, in one of the longest and most beautiful speeches to be found in the Old Testament. He offers a nearly point-for-point reversal of what he and his brothers did to Joseph, and gives the first account we have heard of the depth of his father's grief. He will sell himself as a slave in place of the son of his mother's rival. In fact, 'Judah so feels for his father that he begs to sacrifice himself for a brother more loved than himself' (Meir Sternberg, *The Poetics of Biblical Narrative*,

p. 308). Only such an explicit unsolicited response could convince Joseph of Judah's sincere contrition.

2 Joseph's revelation

Genesis 45

Joseph's response to his brothers is prophetic. Three times (vv. 5, 7–8) he assures them that it was God, not they, who brought him down to Egypt. On one level, this repetition is required to convince the dumbfounded brothers that he is not bitter and doesn't blame them. On another, Joseph's words foreshadow a greater deliverance than the one from this present famine. God has essentially brought them there to initiate the exodus prophesied to Abraham (15:13–14). Even the way in which the brothers leave Egypt foreshadows the later exodus. In verse 18, we find Joseph promising that the 'best of Egypt is yours'. This, like many prophecies, finds immediate as well as later, greater fulfilment. It looks ahead to the booty that the Egyptians will bestow upon the departing Israelite slaves in Exodus 11:2–3 and 12:35–36.

These statements also raise the issue of the interplay between divine sovereignty and human choice. We have here an example of God's purposes being both behind and in conflict with human designs. In selling Joseph, the brothers wanted to be rid of their uppity brat of a brother, who embodied their father's unfair preference, yet God used this action to keep them all alive, along with the people of many other nations.

However, God's interest in their survival hardly exhausts the extent of his purposes. His hand is seen in the protection, promotion and preservation of Joseph and of others through him, but he also addresses the discord and strife brought about by Jacob's favouritism. Jacob's sons must come to terms with this favouritism, not by removing the object of their father's special love or changing his mind about it, but by accepting it and loving him despite it.

These sorts of purposes are only resolved *through* human choices. Joseph had to choose what to do with his brothers once they came to Egypt: he could have exacted revenge but chose not to. The brothers could have left Simeon to rot in an Egyptian jail. Judah could have broken his promise about Benjamin. Jacob could have refused to leave the promised land. All these choices represent uncoerced human responses to divine initiatives, whether of forgiveness, contrition, self-denial or faith. These choices work in conjunction with God's providential interventions to make up the grand design of his purposes in the story—the reconciliation of his people, a faithful reliance on him, and a God-like compassion for others above oneself.

3 The blessing of Pharaoh

Genesis 46:1–7, 26–34; 47:1–31

Genesis 46:2–4 is the only time that God speaks in the Joseph story. His voice is required here to let Jacob know that it is all right to go to Egypt, away from the land in which he was promised an inheritance. Distancing ourselves from the things that God has promised is foolish and faithless, unless we are moving toward God himself.

Notably, when Jacob talks with Pharaoh, he neither refers to himself as 'your servant' nor speaks formally in the third person. Because of his advanced age, he is held in respect, even by the king of Egypt. Pharaoh's honouring of Jacob and his sons represents a partial fulfilment of the Abrahamic blessing: 'those who bless you will be blessed' (Genesis 12:3). Pharaoh is indeed blessed by Jacob's son Joseph, as he gains all of the land of Egypt, except the priests' allowance, along with an annual tribute of a fifth of the land's produce.

Taking an oath in the Ancient Near East was often done by holding an object, much like placing a hand on the Bible in a courtroom. By putting his hand under Jacob's thigh (47:29), Joseph was touching his genitals. In his oath, this symbolised God as the source of life, as well as the sign of his covenant—circumcision. Hence, Joseph was essentially swearing not only on the one who had sired him, but upon God and his covenant. Joseph's promise and its fulfilment thus became the working out of his own faith by honouring God and his promises to his ancestors (Wenham, p. 141).

Why was it so important for Joseph to promise to bring Jacob's bones back to Canaan? The patriarchs show consistent concern for the fulfilment of the Abrahamic blessing, including the promise of land. This explains why Abraham sought a wife for Isaac from his own people and why Jacob insisted on being buried in the land promised to Abraham. This is why it took a divine word to bring him to Egypt. The move to Egypt was a sign of faith in the Abrahamic promises, and so it was seen as temporary, even though he would die in Egypt.

4 Jacob's blessings (I)

Genesis 48

Jacob initially blesses his son Joseph, but several themes run on from this blessing, including the name of God, the recipients, and the land itself.

God is named as *Shaddai* (v. 3). This term is thought to be related to mountains or breasts, and is often translated as 'Almighty'. *El Shaddai*, 'God Almighty,' is always used in conjunction with promises of descendants. In Genesis, where the main characters are often unable to have children, 'it contains the idea that *El Shaddai* is the God who so constrains nature that it does His will, even to the point of making the barren fertile' (Franz Delitzsch, *A New Commentary on Genesis*, Vol. 2, p. 32). Jewish scholars considered it to mean 'One who is sufficient'.

When Jacob blesses Joseph, he actually blesses Joseph's sons, who are then considered full-fledged heirs of Jacob, along with his other eleven sons. In this way, he gives Joseph a double portion, typically reserved for the eldest, who would use it to provide for the family. In seeking for his name and that of his fathers to live on in the boys, Jacob is both commending them as inheritors of the divine promises and commissioning them to seek the fulfilment of those promises.

Jacob mentions Rachel's death on the way to Bethlehem (v. 7). This curious insertion serves two purposes. On the one hand, he is telling Joseph where his mother is buried. On the other, he is expressing his desire to be buried with her in Canaan. Even to the end, Jacob looks forward to the fulfilment of the promises made to Abraham, Isaac and himself.

As for Joseph, Jacob passes on the same promise that God has made to him—that God will be with him and bring him back to the land promised to his forefathers. Jacob actually already owns some land in Canaan, which he bought from the Shechemites (33:18–19). In fact, the Hebrew word in verse 22 for the 'portion' that Jacob gives to Joseph is *Shechem*. Despite the slaughter there and Jacob's subsequent flight from the area (34:1—35:5), Joshua and the Israelites are later able to worship there without having to conquer the land (Joshua 24:1–32). Jacob is eventually buried there, as is Joseph after the exodus (Joshua 24:32). Throughout his blessing, including the mention of his wife and of the land, Jacob consistently keeps his eyes, and the eyes of Joseph, on the prize—the fulfilment of God's promises to Abraham.

5 Jacob's blessings (2)

Genesis 49:1–12

Although Jacob addresses Reuben, his firstborn, in terms that are usually used of God ('outstanding in majesty and power', v. 3), he also predicts Reuben's downfall, the consequence of sleeping with Jacob's concubine. No judge, king or prophet descends from Reuben.

Simeon and Levi, the next in line, are called brothers not because they are related by blood, but because they shed it together (v. 5). Jacob's curse predicts their dispersal (v. 7). The Levites were scattered in 48 cities around Israel (Joshua 21:41), and Simeon was eventually subsumed within Judah's territory (Joshua 19:1–9).

Because these three sons dishonoured their father, the primary blessing falls to the fourth. Judah's blessing (vv. 8–12) has incurred the most debate, and is divided into three main parts—his ascendency, his lion-like nature, and the future leader from his tribe.

Jacob begins by talking of Judah in terms of Joseph's dream for himself: all his brothers will bow down to him. He then describes Judah as a lion. Common in Palestine in biblical times, and often used as royal imagery, lions were seen as the most dominant of beasts (Proverbs 30:30). The allusion in Jacob's blessing is to a lion so indomitable that no one dares attack it, even while it is resting from devouring its prey.

'Shiloh' (v. 10, NASB) is a difficult word to translate, as it can refer to a place, person or phrase. The town of Shiloh is in Ephraim and housed the tabernacle for a short period, but this fits neither the grammar nor the context. Shiloh as a personal name is otherwise unattested. Hence, most scholars render it as 'the one to whom [the sceptre] belongs'. This accords well with ancient versions and Jewish exegesis, which saw a reference to a messianic figure here.

The sceptre is located 'between his feet', a phrase that probably refers to the genitals, indicating that a descendant of Judah would always be leader over Israel. The fact that the sceptre will not depart 'until' the coming of this leader does not mean that a descendant from Judah will stop reigning, but that the leader will have continuity with, and signify the culmination of, Judah's rule (Kenneth Matthews, *Genesis 11:27—50:26*, p. 895).

Leaders used donkeys during the time of the Judges, and Zechariah 9:9 predicts that the Messiah will ride one. The leader in Jacob's blessing ties a donkey and its colt to a vine, which signifies his surpassing wealth, as he is unconcerned about the grapes that the donkeys will consume.

6 Joseph's forgiveness

Genesis 50:15–26

Now that their father is dead, the brothers appeal to Joseph, using the term 'your father' rather than 'our father'. This makes the case more personal for Joseph and avoids elevating themselves to the same level as him. They also bow down to him (v. 18), fulfilling the dreams he shared with them as a boy. This is not a coincidental fulfilment, but an intentional acknowledgement that Joseph was right.

Joseph's response is perhaps the most famous verse in the story (v. 20). It is often cited in connection with divine providence, but in context it refers to Joseph's reason for not exacting revenge on his brothers. Although he rhetorically asks if he is in God's place, ironically he actually does possess the power to let the brothers live or die. However, he assumes that, if God preserved life through their wickedness, he is not the one to judge them for it.

This may seem to infer that Joseph thought God made his brothers sell him into slavery, but the Hebrew literally says, 'You [Joseph's brothers] devised evil against me; God devised it for good—the preservation of many people.' The 'it' that God devises refers not to the sojourn in Egypt but to the 'evil' that the brothers devised. Thus, it does not say that God made them do what they did, only that he took what they did and 'made' it into good. This compares well with Romans 8:28, another often-misquoted verse. This verse does not say that God creates all things for our good, but that he uses all things (whether originally malicious or benevolent) for the good of those who love him and are called according to his purpose.

Finally, although both Abraham's and Jacob's wills were executed, Joseph's is not. The story closes with his body in a coffin in Egypt. Of the promises to Abraham, there is no land, no great multitude of descendants and no great reputation. There is already a blessing to other nations, but perhaps the greatest blessing is to the family itself, which has found healing and unity (see Psalm 133:1). This raises questions about what will happen to the family, to Joseph's body and to the promises of God, anticipating the themes of the next book, Exodus.

Guidelines

The story of Judah confronts us, again, with the consequences of unjust favouritism. How do we deal with this in our own lives? Our response might be one of two types. First, like Joseph's brothers, we might focus on the one who we feel is robbing us of the love, respect, position or material things that we think we are due. This, however, never seems to satisfy, and often merely perpetuates the cycle of abuse. The other route is to try to change the mind of the father, mother, boss, hero, or friend whose favour we seek. This rarely, if ever, succeeds. Judah eventually finds a way forward by focusing his concern on the very one who has not shown concern for him—his father, Jacob. In this way, he refuses to allow the way he was treated to define him, and he rises up to become a true leader in Israel. How can we refocus our complaints into compassion for those who have slighted us?

Joseph's story points to God's providence as a source of hope: even the worst-case scenarios can be conformed to his purposes. However, God's providence does not render human action meaningless. The brothers' deeds, though redeemed, were not erased. Reuben still lost out on the rights of the firstborn; Jacob missed seeing his son grow up; the brothers experienced profound shame. How do we view the evil that befalls us? Do we blame God? Or do we perhaps assume that God's providence makes our own actions inconsequential?

This perspective can be extremely helpful in comforting those who are suffering pain or loss. Rather than subverting the anguish by assigning the calamity to God's will, we can say that what was done was truly evil. It was not of God, and it is appropriate to question and rage against the pain and grief it has caused. However, we also can affirm that the loss does not render us beyond hope or purpose. God is with us even when we feel furthest from his protection, and he accomplishes his good intentions despite the worst that can be devised against us.

FURTHER READING

www.biblearchaeology.org/post/2010/03/04/Joseph-in-Egypt-Part-III.aspx

Victor P. Hamilton, *The Book of Genesis Chapters 18—50* (NICOT), Eerdmans, 1995.

Kenneth A. Matthews, *Genesis 11:27—50:26* (NAC), Broadman and Holman, 2005.

Gordon Wenham, *Genesis 16—50* (WBC), Word, 1994.

Mark 12:13—16:20

Earlier this year Guidelines explored the first two thirds of Mark's Gospel, Mark 1—12, in two separate sections. Over the course of the next three weeks we will turn our attention to the final third of the Gospel, looking particularly at the events surrounding Jesus' death and resurrection.

One of the main characteristics of Mark's Gospel is that it charges along at a fast pace, from its first grand statement that this is 'the beginning of the good news of Jesus Christ, Son of God' to Jesus' calling of his first disciples; from Jesus' opening conflicts with the Jewish leaders to his struggles to get the disciples to comprehend who he was; from his challenging teaching about the costly nature of discipleship to the dawning realisation that Jesus himself was about to live out what it meant to walk the way of the cross.

Mark is a Gospel of two halves, with two major themes: discipleship and the way of the cross. In the first half (up to about chapter 9), the dominant theme is the nature of discipleship, accompanied by the subtheme of the way of the cross. At the Gospel's midpoint these two themes swap over, so that the way of the cross becomes the dominant theme and the nature of discipleship its accompanying subtheme.

As a result, in these final chapters the shadow of the cross becomes almost our entire focus. As we rejoin Mark in chapter 12, it is Jesus' increasing conflict with various different Jewish groups that focuses our attention on the gathering storm ahead.

Quotations are taken from the New Revised Standard Version of the Bible.

21–27 September

1 Should we pay taxes?

Mark 12:13–17

Mark 12 is a chapter of conflict. As we watch, various different groups approach Jesus in an attempt to trip him up. Mark suggests that this enmity emerged from Jesus' telling of the parable of the tenants in the verses just before these ones (12:1–12). Verse 12 observed that the leaders realised that Jesus was talking about them; they wanted to arrest him but were afraid of the crowd.

The arguments that unfold in the rest of chapter 12 appear to be trying to work out who Jesus was aligning himself with. This first conversation, in verses 13–17, is about politics. One of the hot topics of Jesus' day was about whether or not Jews ought to pay taxes to Rome as well as to the temple. The problem was that the temple tax—payable to the temple authorities once a year by all adult males—was intended to be a complete tax. After the invasion of the Romans, the temple tax continued at the same rate but was supplemented by an additional tax to the Roman authorities. This was a burden that, for many people, proved too much. Galileans, in particular, had the reputation of rebelling against Roman taxation and Roman rule in general. Lying behind this conversation, then, is the question of whether Jesus would align himself with rebellious Galilean groups who sought to drive the Romans from the land.

It is worth noting the unusual alliance between the Pharisees and the Herodians in this story. The Pharisees and Herodians were not natural allies. The Pharisees were largely concerned with purity and how to live out daily life as devoutly as possible; the Herodians (or followers of the Herod family) were appeasers of the Romans and were despised for it by most devout Jews, especially the Pharisees. However, there is evidence that both groups supported paying taxes to Rome, seeing it as an acceptable price to pay for peace, so they were united upon this one issue, and were probably using it in an attempt to discover whether they could claim that Jesus was anti-Roman.

2 A complicated marriage

Mark 12:18–27

The second question to Jesus comes from the Sadducees and focuses on the knotty issue of beliefs about life after death. In some ways it is a shame that this question was asked by the Sadducees simply in order to trick Jesus. Jesus does not talk very much about life after death and to have some unforced teaching from him about the nature of the resurrection life would have been very helpful indeed.

We are alerted to the fact that this is a trick question by Mark's reminder that the Sadducees said there would be no resurrection (v. 18). The basis of their question was a farce since they did not believe that resurrection was possible anyway. The Sadducees were a group of Jews in the first century who were particularly associated with temple worship and were largely aristocratic. There is not much known about them (other than that they did not believe in resurrection) but we do know that they strongly opposed the Pharisees, who did believe in resurrection.

The question they are really asking Jesus here is about whether he aligns himself with the Pharisees or not (which is ironic, given that Jesus has been in direct conflict with the Pharisees in the previous passage). The question is based on a principle known as levirate marriage, the rules of which were laid out in Deuteronomy 25:5–10. Levirate marriage was designed to protect widows and to ensure that they could be kept within the financial care of the family into which they had married.

Jesus' answer to the question is to tell the Sadducees that they are mistaken (v. 24). The problem, it seems, is that they are beginning in entirely the wrong place. Their assumption is that the same rules will govern the new age as govern this age. In the ancient world, the main focus of marriage was property and inheritance, so to be 'like the angels in heaven' (v. 25) means that people's focus in the new age will be the eternal worship of God, not who inherits what income.

Jesus' final observation leaves us in no doubt of his views about life after death. God is the God of the living, and he is also (still) the God of Abraham, Isaac and Jacob. It is clear, then, that these people are alive and the Sadducees are wrong in their conclusion that there is no life after death.

3 Which is the best commandment?

Mark 12:28–34

The next interrogator of Jesus is a lawyer, and it is somewhat surprising that, in Mark's account here, he is not a combative character. As we have already seen, there has been much conflict so far in this chapter between Jesus, the Pharisees, the Herodians and the Sadducees. In addition, the versions of this story found in Matthew and Luke present the lawyer as attempting to 'test' Jesus (Matthew 22:35; Luke 10:25). If we consider, too, that the scribes are never presented well in Mark's Gospel, the positive presentation of this lawyer comes as something of a surprise.

It might be that the trickiness or otherwise of a question lies in the eye of the beholder and that, whereas Matthew and Luke both considered this a trick question, Mark thought it was genuine. It might even be that, in all of the conversations between Jesus and the Jewish groups, we are seeing something more like a robust rabbinic conversation than an attempt to trip Jesus up. Nevertheless, we cannot avoid the knowledge that, in Mark, all of these encounters take place in the last week of Jesus' life and, as a result, form part of the backdrop to his death.

This particular conversation concerns the main focus of the law. The answer, famously, has both a vertical and horizontal component: love of God and love of neighbour. There is much discussion among scholars about whether Jesus was the first to formulate the summary of the law exactly like this (a discussion made more heated by the fact that, in Luke 10:27, the summary is on the lips of the lawyer, not Jesus). It is important, however, not to be too sidetracked by this question. The recognition that following the law properly involves both a vertical and a horizontal dimension goes all the way back to the Old Testament prophets. Throughout history, human beings have tended to place more emphasis on one than the other and we have always needed constant reminders of the importance of keeping the two together.

One of the most significant features of this story is the fact that Jesus reinforces this double dynamic. Love of God and love of neighbour stand at the heart of the kingdom of God: no wonder Jesus declared that the lawyer was not far from it.

4 Son of David or Son of God?

Mark 12:35–44

This chapter of hard questions ends with one final hard question, this time from Jesus himself. It is quite possible that this passage should really begin with 12:34b—'After that no one dared to ask him any question'—the idea being that Jesus outwitted all his conversation partners and, in the silence engendered by his responses, asked a hard question of his own.

It is truly a hard question, and its meaning is not entirely clear. There is no doubt that we are to understand Jesus as saying something important about his Messiahship, but the question is: what was he saying? One possibility is that he was opposing the idea that the Messiah was the 'Son of David', but this makes little sense, since the title 'Son of David' is used of Jesus without dispute elsewhere in Mark (10:47–48). It is more likely that Jesus was tackling the statement that the Messiah is 'only' the Son of David and nothing more. If David himself calls him 'Lord', then we should too. Jesus was indeed a Son of David but he was also the Son of God and, as such, deserved the title 'Lord'.

In the midst of these complex, high-level political and theological questions, we find something very different—the account of a widow sacrificially giving as much as she could. At first glance, this little story appears somewhat out of place. In reality, however, it gives us the key to understanding the whole of the chapter. Beneath the questions lies one simple issue: how should people respond to God and his Son, Jesus Christ? The Pharisees, Herodians and Sadducees had bound up their responses in such complex political and theological thinking that they had forgotten what God really requires. All that he does require is what the widow offered—a simple, heartfelt but generous response to the God who has poured out his riches on us. In the midst of the complexity of the questions swirling around Jesus, Mark reminds us of a theme that has been present throughout the Gospel: the key issue is simply our response to God and to Jesus.

5 Holding fast in the midst of chaos

Mark 13:1–13

The next chapter of Mark's Gospel takes us into very different material. It is the biggest block of teaching by Jesus in this part of the Gospel and it is, for many people, bemusing and hard to comprehend. This is for good reason. Mark 13 contains Jesus' most sustained teaching about the future and what it holds. It is often termed 'apocalyptic' or 'a mini apocalypse' because it is reminiscent of the book of Revelation (otherwise known as 'the Apocalypse').

Mark 13 is confusing, however, because it is not entirely clear what it is describing. The second half of the chapter, in particular, refers to cosmic events, like the sun darkening and the Son of Man coming in clouds, while the first half refers to something that seems much closer to a historical event (such as the fall of the Jerusalem temple in AD70). There is little agreement among scholars about whether this chapter is to be understood primarily in terms of the fall of Jerusalem or primarily in terms of the 'end times'. My own view is that it refers to both, and represents Jesus' teaching about how his faithful disciples are to act in the face of the world-changing, life-changing events that threaten to swamp them.

If we recognise this, then the chapter becomes an absolutely vital guide for Christian living. It is tempting to believe that our lives as Christians should be tranquil idylls of peace and harmony, but Mark 13 turns this expectation on its head. As followers of Jesus, we must expect upset and tumult, conflict and dishonesty. The question is not about whether such upset will occur; it is about how we will behave in the face of such events.

Jesus' teaching on this is clear. Our vocation as followers of Jesus is to be people of faithfulness, steadfastness and endurance. No matter what chaos swirls around us, we are to hold fast to the truth that we have encountered in Jesus (13:5–6). No matter what hostility we face, we must trust the Holy Spirit to give us the words to bear witness to Jesus when we need them the most (v. 11). Most of all, though, we must hold on to the end (v. 13).

6 The signs of the times

Mark 13:14–29

Mark 13:14–29 is even more closely focused on action than yesterday's passage. Jesus' teaching here concentrates on the ability to recognise what is happening when it happens and to act accordingly. There is no doubt in his mind that these cataclysmic events are on their way and, indeed, are linked to his forthcoming death. People's attitudes to Jesus, Son of God, are symptomatic of their attitudes in general, and the ripples that began at Jesus' death on the cross will continue outwards to the fall of Jerusalem in AD70 and beyond. The appropriate attitude of Jesus' followers is not to hope that these events will not happen, but to expect them and act accordingly.

It is worth noticing that this is a key discipleship theme, running throughout Mark. The ability to recognise the nature of what is really going on, to understand it in the light of the good news of Jesus Christ, Son of God, and to act accordingly, is one of Mark's key strands of discipleship. This theme reaches its climax in verse 28. Jesus' followers are adept at recognising what it means when fig trees come into leaf; they should become equally adept at reading the 'signs of the times' and of working out what those signs mean about how they should behave.

It is here that this passage becomes profoundly relevant for today. Much of Mark 13 can seem as if it has little to say to us today, as it is focused on events that took place around the fall of the temple in AD70. Underneath the passage, however, is a powerful message. Disciples of Jesus are not just to be swept along on the tide of events around them. Instead, they should become astute readers of what is going on, able to interpret the significance of the events that unfold around them and able to respond with faithfulness, love and witness, no matter what happens.

Guidelines

This week's passages are a bit of a motley collection, covering a wide range of subjects, from taxation to levirate marriage, and from Jesus' identity as the Son of David/Son of God to future cataclysm. Beneath this wide variety of themes, however, lies a vital message about the importance of clear vision and wise judgement in the face of conflict and chaos. Jesus' conflict and conversation with the various different Jewish leaders models the kind of attitudes that he tells his disciples to adopt, in chapter 13. His point is that in the midst of the chaos, uncertainty and anxiety that is sure to come their way in the years following his death, they should stay strong and focused. They must not be pulled this way and that by people who falsely claim to be messiahs; they must not be stunned into silence by terror or caught off guard by surprising events. In chapter 12, Jesus modelled exactly this way of being.

Today, the chaos that most of us face is of a very different kind, but Jesus' teaching remains as important for us as for his first disciples. The life of discipleship must be shaped by clarity of vision, faithfulness and endurance. The need for these qualities does not change, even though the circumstances do.

1 Keep awake

Mark 13:30–37

This passage contains one of the most controversial of all of Jesus' sayings: 'Truly I tell you, this generation will not pass away until all these things have taken place' (v. 30). Over the years, fierce debate has raged, and continues to rage, about how we should interpret this saying. The centre of the storm focuses on two questions: did Jesus actually say these words (or has Mark put them on his lips) and, whoever said them, are they right or wrong?

Some scholars think that Jesus expected 'the end' to come in his own lifetime and died disillusioned because it had not happened. Some think that these words reflect the early church's belief that 'the end' would happen before the first disciples died—a view that they had to readjust when it did not occur. Others think that the phrase 'all these things' refers solely to the fall of the temple in AD70, in which case the prophecy that 'this generation will not pass away until all these things have taken place' did, in fact, come true. Each person must come to their own view on the accuracy of what Jesus said here, but my own view is that Jesus was talking about the terrible chaos and catastrophe that happens when societies descend into war. All these things certainly happened at the fall of Jerusalem. They have happened throughout history and continue to happen today. They will also take place at the end of all times.

In my view, Jesus' teaching here was true then and continues to be true. We simply do not know when such catastrophe will strike us and the societies in which we live. We only need to look around the world today to see how true this is. The lives of people in Syria, for example, have gone from peaceful prosperity to the nightmare of chaos and destruction in the space of only a few years. As Jesus says, we do not know when the time will come—whether that time be a period of destruction or the destruction that marks the end times. Therefore, we should keep awake, stay alert and be ready to respond whenever it comes.

2 In memory of her

Mark 14:1–11

One of the big questions about the last week of Jesus' life concerns what it was that made Judas betray Jesus. Luke and John suggest that the devil was involved in his decision (Luke 22:3; John 13:2), but John also notes that Judas was unhappy at the extravagance of Mary's anointing of Jesus' feet (John 12:5).

It is worth noting that the anointing in Mark 14:3–9 was probably a different event from the anointing in John 12: it took place at Simon the leper's house, not Mary and Martha's; Jesus was anointed by an unnamed woman, not by Mary; his head was anointed, not his feet. Nevertheless, like John, Mark associates its extravagance with Judas' decision to betray Jesus. His placing of the narrative between the Jewish leaders' renewed determination to kill Jesus (vv. 1–2) and Judas' decision to betray him (vv. 10–11) certainly suggests that Mark thinks there is a connection to be made.

The question is: what is the connection? John 12:6 suggests that Judas was corrupt and resented the use of money that he could have used elsewhere, but Mark does not. The implication of Mark's account is simply that the event confirmed to Judas that he did not fit as a follower of Jesus. This feeling might have been connected with money; it might have reflected a sense of disillusionment that Jesus' ministry was neither primarily revolutionary nor focused solely on the care of the poor. Some people have even suggested that Judas' problem arose from the fact that he was from the south, whereas the other disciples were all from Galilee. In reality, we will never know what made Judas betray Jesus, although something about the woman's action and Jesus' response to her tipped him over the edge.

It was certainly an extravagant action: nard comes from the spikenard plant, which can only be harvested from the foothills of the Himalayas and was very expensive. The importance of the woman's action—rather like that of the widow (12:42)—was its overwhelming generosity. In contrast with all of Jesus' other interactions in this last week of his life, which were based on protecting the right and power of those talking to him, the woman responded from her heart with joy and generosity. She was the icon of true discipleship and revealed in her response to Jesus the paucity of other people's responses.

3 This is my body

It is intriguing to notice that here, as in Mark 11:1–3, Jesus appears to have made arrangements before his arrival. In 11:1–3 he has arranged the loan of a donkey for his entry into Jerusalem; here he has arranged the loan of a room for the Passover meal. The pre-booking of a room for the Passover meal was common sense. There is disagreement about how many people would have gone to Jerusalem for the Passover but the most conservative estimate is 180,000, which, for a normal population of 30,000, is an enormous influx of people. The prearranged room therefore indicates just how much importance Jesus placed on his last Passover meal with his disciples.

One of the most iconic of all the Gospel narratives is the story of Jesus' last supper with his disciples. In both Luke's account (Luke 22:7–20) and Paul's (1 Corinthians 11:23–25), Jesus commands his disciples to 'do this in remembrance of me'; making this one of only two direct commands that he gave (the other being that we should love one another, John 13:34–35). In Mark's version, however, Jesus does not tell his disciples to eat and drink in remembrance of him. Mark focuses our attention much more on the meal as a Passover meal and as the marker of the inauguration of a new covenant.

The words that Jesus speaks in Mark, 'This is my body… This is my blood' (vv. 22, 24) are particularly reminiscent of the words spoken at the Passover meal: 'This is the bread of affliction'. As we read Jesus' accompanying statement, 'This is my blood of the covenant, which is poured out for many', we become aware that, in Mark's mind, the last supper inaugurates a new era. Just as the daubing of the blood of the lambs on the doorposts and the subsequent flight from Egypt inaugurated a new level of relationship with God that was lived out in the Mosaic covenant, so the last supper inaugurated a relationship that would be lived out in the new covenant. Just as the Jews looked back to that night as they celebrated the Passover meal to remind them of God's covenant with them, so also the last supper reminds us of God's new covenant of love.

4 Pray that you do not come to the time of trial

Mark 14:26–42

After the last supper, Jesus and his disciples went out to the Mount of Olives, to a place that both Matthew and Mark identify with the Aramaic name 'Gethsemane'. John 18:1 calls it a garden but not Gethsemane, so all these references put together give us the common name 'garden of Gethsemane'. It is likely to have been in the foothills of the Mount of Olives, just outside Jerusalem. Gethsemane means 'olive press', so it may well have been the location where the mountain's olives were pressed to extract the oil.

It is clear from all the Gospels that Jesus' usual place to stay near Jerusalem was Bethany, at the top of the mountain. However, for major festivals, an extended boundary was set around Jerusalem, beyond which people were not allowed to travel during the festival, and Bethany would have fallen outside that boundary. Therefore, Jesus and his disciples found a new place to stay for the duration of the festival. This was why the Jewish leaders needed someone like Judas to betray Jesus, as otherwise they would not have known where to find him.

The narrative from the end of the last supper to Jesus' arrest sums up in perfect miniature the challenge of discipleship that Mark has been exploring throughout the whole of his Gospel. It also reminds us not to judge Judas too harshly, since, in the end, all of the disciples betrayed Jesus by running off and leaving him (14:50). Mark reminds us in this sharply drawn account that there is a world of difference between what we want to believe about our own discipleship and the reality. Peter was determined to be recognised as someone who would not fail and would not leave Jesus (v. 29) but immediately broke his word, first by falling asleep (v. 37) and later by actively denying Jesus.

It is here that Jesus' words to Peter become so important: 'Keep awake and pray that you may not come into the time of trial; the spirit indeed is willing, but the flesh is weak' (v. 38). Jesus' clear-sighted observation is that our intentions and the reality often do not match, and that it is better for us if our intentions are not tested. Peter, sadly, slept rather than praying that he might avoid temptation; later he discovered to his cost why this prayer was so important.

5 Seated at the right hand of power

Mark 14:43–65

The problem for the Jewish authorities, which we have seen from chapter 12 onwards, comes to a head with Jesus' arrest and trial. Their opposition to Jesus has been growing throughout the previous two chapters but they do not have sufficient grounds to arrest or condemn him. Mark's account of Jesus' arrest and trial make this clear: they are fumbling for an excuse to justify their actions.

Their first attempted justification is suggested by the manner in which they approach Jesus in the garden: he asks them why they have come to arrest him as though he were 'a bandit' (v. 48). The Greek word *lestes* was a very specific word used to describe those who were politically motivated freedom-fighters, many of whom came from Galilee. The irony of this particular accusation is that Jesus is eventually crucified between two such bandits, bringing full circle the suggestion that this is how the Jewish authorities wanted to portray him. The reality, as Jesus points out, is that nothing could be further from the truth: his actions are simply those of a rabbi, teaching daily in the temple.

The disarray of the Jewish leaders is further emphasised during Jesus' trial: the leaders do not have a substantial charge against Jesus, so the many accusations they have lined up do not match or, indeed, make much sense. The turning point in the trial is the brief exchange between Jesus and the high priest (vv. 60–62). It is this exchange that appears to give them what they need in order to hand him over to the Romans. On the surface, it seems to be linked to Jesus' acknowledgement of the suggestion that he is the Messiah. The problem with this, however, is that there were many characters claiming messianic status in the first century, none of whom were treated with the ire that is directed at Jesus.

Much more inflammatory, triggering the accusation of blasphemy, are Jesus' next words—that they will see the Son of Man sitting at the right hand of the Power. The claim to be sitting in the heavenly realms with God is a claim of divinity and, as such, would deserve the label of blasphemy in the eyes of the Jewish leaders. In any case, it is enough to confirm that they have grounds to hand him over to the Romans and death.

6 I do not know him

Mark 14:66–72

The story of Peter's betrayal of Jesus remains very popular. Part of the reason for this is that, although shocking in effect, it is really rather mundane. It is not a spectacular event, just a rather sad, hole-in-the-corner denial of friendship and discipleship—and this is what makes it so easy for us to understand. Betrayal so often creeps up on us in ordinary situations rather than at moments of great drama and crisis.

In fairness to Peter, however, we need to acknowledge that this was a moment of crisis for him. The world as he knew it had just been turned on its head; the leader he had followed had been taken and the future was bleak—but the actual context of his denial was unspectacular. He was in a courtyard, not a court room; he was questioned by servants and bystanders, not anyone in authority; he was asked simply about his affiliation with Jesus, not his views or his actions. Even in this context, though, and with three opportunities given to him to acknowledge Jesus, he found himself unable even to admit that he knew him.

It is striking to notice that we call Judas 'the betrayer'. On one level this is justified, as he was the person who made the arrest of Jesus possible, but Peter's denial was every bit as much a betrayal of Jesus. Judas may have handed him over but he at least acknowledged his connection with him. The famous 'betrayer's kiss' in Gethsemane is thought by many to have been simply the traditional greeting between a rabbi and his disciple (although it also served to identify Jesus to the crowd). In other words, Judas, while handing Jesus over, at least acknowledged his own connection with him; Peter refused to do even that.

Unlike in the other Gospels, both Judas' and Peter's stories stop here. In Mark, we learn nothing of Judas' demise (see Matthew 27:3–5; Acts 1:18–19) or of Peter's restoration (John 21:15–19). Nevertheless, I can't help wondering what Jesus might have said to Judas if he had lived until the resurrection. Would he, like Peter, have been forgiven? Of course, we will never know, but it is hard not to wonder about it.

Guidelines

This week's readings circled around faithfulness and betrayal. They began with Jesus' command to keep awake because we do not know when the master will return, with all its implications about the need to remain faithful. We saw Judas starting out on a slippery slope to betrayal. We saw the disciples all protesting their determination not to betray Jesus, and all, without exception, running away—with Peter, whose protests were the loudest, actually denying that he had ever met Jesus at all.

In all of these stories, just one person not only remained faithful but also demonstrated that faithfulness in her actions. The woman who anointed Jesus' head acted with great extravagance and, in doing so, demonstrated heartfelt faithfulness. She acted out of the depths of her love in response to the depths of who Jesus was. Jesus recognised this and praised her action because of it.

This reminds us of the deep challenges of true and faithful discipleship. True discipleship is to be found in steadfastness, not anxiety or fear; it is to be discerned in heartfelt response, not in good intention. Most of all, it is to be found in an abiding love of the one who is love. Mark's Gospel continues to challenge us, as it has done time and time again since chapter 1, to respond to Jesus Christ, Son of God—and, having responded, to live out our choice faithfully, no matter how great the cost.

5–11 October

1 Crucify him

Mark 15:1–15

The account of Jesus' trial before Pilate focuses our attention on the panic that Jesus has evoked in the Jewish leaders. Mark, alongside the other Gospel writers, is keen to remind us that Pilate was highly reluctant to condemn Jesus and did everything in his power to avoid doing so. Given Pilate's reputation, this is ironic. Pilate was well known for his brutality and was criticised for it by both Philo and Josephus, leading Jewish writers of the first century. Indeed, Pilate's brutality was so great that, in the end, he was summoned back to Rome in around AD37 (only a few years after the death of Jesus), after his vicious suppression of a Samaritan uprising.

It appears, therefore, that Pilate's reluctance to crucify Jesus was not due to his fine character or his passion for justice, but may well have been because he did not perceive Jesus as a threat. The torturously slow death of a crucifixion was designed not just as a means of execution but also as a deterrent to others who might follow the same path. The fact that Pilate did not want to crucify Jesus, and did not seek out Jesus' other followers afterwards, suggests that, unlike the Jewish leaders, he did not think that Jesus was dangerous.

We are left, then, to work out what it was that made the Jewish leaders so clearly terrified of Jesus and his ministry. Mark suggests that their motivation was jealousy (v. 10), but whether or not this explains everything is debatable. The actions of the Jewish leaders suggest more than just jealousy: the speed of the trial, the confused nature of the accusations and the determination in their pleas to Pilate all indicate that they were afraid. Indeed, it must have been the strongest of emotions that would cause them to argue that anyone should be crucified—a mode of execution which was anathema for a Jew (see Deuteronomy 21:23).

So what was it that made them so afraid? Did they fear that Jesus' teaching would unpick their fragile peace with the Romans? Were they concerned that Jesus' identity would challenge their power? Was his claim to divinity unsettling and blasphemous? The answer may well be all of these and more. What we do know is that the very person of Jesus—what he said and how he lived—so terrified the Jewish leaders that they could not rest until he was dead.

2 The father of Alexander and Rufus

Mark 15:16–27

One of the most tantalising figures of this whole narrative is Simon of Cyrene. Mark tells us almost nothing about him while at the same time providing some vitally important details. We know that he came from an ancient city in a part of north Africa that today would be called Libya. We also know that there was a Jewish community in Cyrene, since in Acts 2:10 Jews from Cyrene are present to hear Peter's synagogue sermon.

Simon was probably a devout Jew, visiting Jerusalem for the Passover.

What is less clear is why he was coming in 'from the country' (v. 21). As we noted above, Passover regulations required Jews arriving for the Passover to stay within an extended boundary for the duration of the festival. The 'country' that Mark refers to must have been within this boundary (like the garden of Gethsemane).

Even more powerful is the glancing reference to Simon's two sons, for in that reference lies a world of meaning. Mark names them in apparent confidence that the recipients of his Gospel will know who he is talking about, the implication being that the two sons were well known in the Christian community. This suggests that Simon of Cyrene was no longer an unknown Jew from north Africa but someone whose family followed Jesus. That brief encounter with Jesus at his most vulnerable apparently drew at least some of Simon's family into the Christian community: Simon went from carrying Jesus' cross once to taking up his own daily.

The rest of the crucifixion narrative reminds us of two of the accusations against Jesus: that he was the King of the Jews (vv. 17–19, 26) and that he was a bandit (v. 27). The irony of these two accusations being placed side by side is that they are both profoundly true and profoundly false. Jesus was not just 'King of the Jews' but 'King of the whole world', a message that Mark's Gospel was determined to communicate as clearly and as widely as possible. At the same time, he was not a bandit in the sense that he was attempting to overthrow the Romans and drive them out by force, but the power of his message of self-giving love struck a deathblow to the heart of the Roman principles of achieving peace by military might, and did indeed subvert that mighty empire.

3 A complete revelation

Mark 15:29–39

In each of the Gospels, the crucifixion narrative brings together the many different themes of the Gospel into a seamless whole—and this is true especially in Mark. Throughout the Gospel, the theme of divine revelation has been woven together with the theme of secrecy. At the baptism (1:11) and transfiguration (9:7), God declared that Jesus was his beloved Son, while Jesus told people time and time again to say nothing about who he was and what he had done (see, for example, 1:44).

The moments of great revelation in Mark's Gospel are accompanied by events of great significance: at the baptism, heaven is torn apart, and at the transfiguration a cloud comes down from heaven. (Clouds were a traditional marker of God's presence in the Old Testament: see, for example, Exodus 24:16.) At Jesus' crucifixion, an even greater event takes place: the veil of the temple is torn in two. This veil is almost certainly the veil that separated the Holy of Holies from the rest of the temple. The Holy of Holies was the place where God came to dwell among his people, but it was so holy and his presence so dangerous to those who might behold him inadvertently that only the high priest was able to enter it, and then only once a year.

At Jesus' death, this veil or curtain, Mark tells us, was torn in two from top to bottom (v. 38). The event was much greater than the previous revelations because it implied a more permanent tearing apart. After the baptism, the heavens came back together again; the curtain would be much harder to mend! Just like the tearing of the heavens, it marks a significant moment, and we might expect that, shortly, a voice will speak to proclaim the Sonship of Jesus—as indeed it does. What is remarkable this time, however, is that this is not God's voice but the voice of a centurion, the soldier overseeing Jesus' death. At the moment of grand revelation, it is the very person who needs to hear the message who proclaims it. The revelation is so complete that we no longer need God's own voice to declare who Jesus is: even a Roman soldier now knows his true identity.

4 Not alone

Mark 15:40–47

It is easy to read the story of Jesus' crucifixion and resurrection with such an eye to the high points of the stories that we miss some of the important gems that Mark has scattered along the path. We find two of these in the final verses of chapter 15.

Throughout the crucifixion narrative, we may have assumed that Jesus was alone: the disciples ran away from Gethsemane, Peter denied Jesus in the courtyard, and we have not heard of them since then. The assumption that, at his death, he was profoundly alone is made all the more poignant by his cry, 'My God, my God, why have you forsaken me?' (v. 34, quoting Psalm 22:1). Immediately after Jesus' death, however, Mark pulls the camera back a little from his tight focus on Jesus' last journey and we discover that our assumption was wrong. Jesus was not, in fact, alone. There were a number of women looking on from a distance (v. 40). Some are named, others not; nevertheless they were there with Jesus in his final moments.

The second gem follows on the heels of the first. Writers from the first century declare that very many Jews were crucified by the Romans in the first century, but there are few archaeological remains to support this claim. Victims of crucifixion were left to hang on crosses after their death while their bodies decayed and were consumed by birds of prey. The bones were probably then thrown into a rubbish dump, so it is hardly surprising that there are limited archaeological remains that can prove a cause of death. What is important to notice is that Jesus' body was not left on the cross. It was taken down carefully and buried by Joseph of Arimathea, a member of the Sanhedrin that had handed Jesus over to the Romans in the first place.

The story of Jesus' desolation and isolation, then, has begun to shift. Both physically and emotionally, darkness hung over the land as he died—but, once he was dead, even before Easter Sunday morning dawned, there were some glimmers of light. Jesus was not abandoned: the women had never left. Nor was he left alone: one of the Jewish leaders from the very grouping that had orchestrated his death ensured that his body was cared for and buried. Even before we get to Easter morning, Mark shows us that the darkness was not as dark as we first thought.

5 Go, tell

Mark 16:1–8

One of the oddest features of Mark's Gospel is its ending. Although, in your Bible, chapter 16 may well go on beyond verse 8, most scholars would say that, in its original form, it ended there. If this is true, then the Gospel ends with the rather unexciting words 'So they went out and fled from the tomb, for terror and amazement had seized them; and they said nothing to anyone, for they were afraid.' We can even imagine the earliest readers turning the page, maybe shaking the document to see if there was any more that they had missed.

Many scholars, however, myself included, believe that this oddest of odd endings is indeed Mark's intended ending, and that it brings to a rather wonderful climax one of Mark's most important themes. The key feature of this account is that the young man at the tomb (whose white garments indicate that he is an angel), for the very first time in the whole Gospel, utters the words 'Go, tell' (v. 7). Until this point, people have been constantly told to be quiet and not to say anything, but here the angel breaks that tradition and announces that the moment has come for the women (those who had demonstrated their faithfulness by not leaving Jesus alone at the crucifixion) to proclaim the good news of Jesus risen from the dead.

Yet the women don't proclaim it; they run away, afraid. The rather pleasing irony is that we know they did eventually say something to someone—otherwise we would not be reading today that they didn't! Nevertheless, Mark is making a somewhat stark point about discipleship here. One of the key points of the whole Gospel is that Jesus summons his followers to self-sacrificial discipleship, a discipleship that recognises who he really is and is prepared to take up the cross to follow him.

As we reach the end of Mark's Gospel, the prospects for discipleship look bleak. Jesus' male disciples ran away before the crucifixion; his female ones have just followed them. The call of the Gospel, then, rings out to each one of us: what will you do? Will you run too? Or will you hear the call of Jesus Christ, Son of God, crucified and risen from the dead, and 'go, tell' this good news to the ends of the earth?

6 Mark's ending

Mark 16:9–20

I indicated in the previous comment that many scholars do not think this ending of Mark's Gospel is genuine. The first reason for this is that it is not present in many of the oldest and most reliable manuscripts; the other is that its writing style is significantly different. By now you will be familiar with Mark's sparse language and rapid style of delivery—the way in which he describes the disciples and Jesus' interaction with them. If you look at verses 9–20, you may be able to tell that the writing simply feels different.

Another intriguing feature of these verses is that they feel like a digest of the endings of the other Gospels. We have the tradition that Mary Magdalene saw Jesus first from John's 20:1–18; we have the story of the road to Emmaus from Luke 24:13–33 and the great commission from Matthew 28:16–20. In other words, we have the best bits of the resurrection appearances from each of the other three Gospels, all rolled into one as the ending to Mark. It isn't impossible that Mark did, in fact, write this, but it is at least questionable.

The question you face, therefore, is whether you are persuaded by the argument that verse 8 is the proper ending for the Gospel or whether you feel (as others have clearly felt throughout Christian history) that it could not have ended there. If you do feel like this, various options lie before you. You may decide that Mark ended with what is known as the shorter ending (many versions of the Bible include this as a footnote to Mark 16). The problem is that this feels even less like the style of Mark than the longer ending does. Alternatively, you may accept the longer ending, or you may consider the possibility that Mark ended the Gospel in a different way—a way that is now lost. Each of us needs to decide for ourselves what we think the answer to this conundrum is.

Whatever you do decide, the good news remains the same: the beginning of the good news of Jesus Christ, Son of God, that Mark declared in 1:1 now rolls onwards and outwards from the Gospel. It is to be found wherever anyone hears the call, 'Come, follow me', and leaves what they are doing to follow.

Guidelines

Mark's Gospel, with its twin themes of the call of discipleship and the way of the cross, ends (whether at 16:8 or beyond) with a ringing challenge to each one of us. How will you respond to Jesus' call? Will you, like the Jewish leaders, oppose him at every turn? Will you, like the crowds, follow him in amazement but without a genuine response? Will you, like the earliest disciples, run away when the going gets tough? Or will you, like the widow in 12:42–44 or the unnamed woman in Mark 14:3–9, respond from your heart with generosity and love to the God who loves you? Most importantly of all, will you heed the command of the angel at the tomb to 'Go, tell' the good news of Jesus' resurrection?

One of the lovely features of Mark's Gospel is that although the disciples do not get a very good press in the telling of the story, we know that they came good in the end. The very fact that we can read the Gospel today tells us that the disciples, both male and female, did return and did proclaim the good news of Jesus Christ, Son of God. The question that remains is whether we will too.

FURTHER READING

Elizabeth Malbon, *Hearing Mark: A listener's guide*, Continuum, 2002.

Ben Witherington III, *The Gospel of Mark: Socio-rhetorical commentary*, Eerdmans, 2001.

James Woodward, Paula Gooder and Mark Pryce, *Journeying with Mark*, SPCK, 2011

Tom Wright, *Mark for Everyone*, SPCK, 2001.

1 Samuel

The division of the book of Samuel into 'First' and 'Second' is a practice originally introduced by the Greek translation (the Septuagint), which divided the Hebrew text into two parts. Strangely, though, it called them 1 and 2 Kings, making the subsequent two books 3 and 4 Kings. Before that, the two books of Samuel existed as one and were part of the 'Former Prophets' section of the Jewish canon, which ran from Joshua to 2 Kings. This means that whenever we treat the first book of Samuel separately, we should always keep in mind its second half and the broader context of the books of Kings.

Traditionally the book of Samuel is believed to have been written by the prophets that ministered during that time, the most important being Samuel, followed by Nathan and Gad (1 Chronicles 29:29). Scholars now believe that, although different sources might have come directly from the contemporaries of the prophets, they were brought together by later editors to compile a theological history of Israel from Moses to the destruction of Jerusalem by the Babylonians in 587BC. This editorial work encompasses books from Deuteronomy to 2 Kings and is often called the Deuteronomistic History. What mattered for these editors was the theological evaluation of the entire history through the lens of the covenant found in Deuteronomy 28, where blessings and curses were promised in response to obedience or disobedience. The extent of such editorial work in Samuel continues to be a subject of debate among scholars; however, the overall suggestion provides a good explanation of the theological conclusions found in it.

The main concern in the first part of the book of Samuel is the transition from theocracy to monarchy and what that meant for the role of the Lord as the supreme ruler. As monarchy is established, the aim shifts, providing a prototype in the figure of David of a godly king. But, as the Deuteronomistic History develops beyond Samuel towards the book of Kings, it becomes apparent that the continual failure of monarchy to hold fast to this model is leading the people towards national catastrophe—the exile. Nevertheless, despite its failure, monarchy has already planted the messianic hope that a 'son of David' will one day bring back God's kingdom.

Quotations are taken from the New Revised Standard Version.

1 The rise of Samuel

1 Samuel 1:1–28; 2:22–35

Samuel's birth narrative follows the common Old Testament motif of an important child (such as Isaac, Joseph and Samson) being born of a barren mother (Sarah, Rachel and the wife of Manoah) who is remembered by a gracious God. The child becomes a significant instrument in God's divine plan in the events to come. However, Samuel's birth and his early years are set uniquely in direct contrast to Israel's religious decline at the time, illustrated by Eli's priesthood and the religious centre of Shiloh.

The author highlights the contrast by constantly interweaving these two themes throughout chapters 1—3, setting Samuel and his mother in apposition with Eli and his children. So, great attention is given to the sacrifices and religious duties that Samuel's family performs faithfully, while Eli's sons are described as abusing their priestly duties; Hannah's fervent prayer is met by Eli's lack of insight; Hannah's plea not to be misunderstood as a 'worthless woman' ('daughter of Beliyaal', an unusual Hebrew phrase) points sarcastically to Eli's failure to control his sons, the real scoundrels ('sons of Beliyaal' in Hebrew). Eli's lack of insight takes on a further spiritual dimension in chapter 3, where his old age and dim eyes echo the lack of visions from God in the land (3:1), contrasted with a young and inexperienced Samuel who brings back the visions and the prophetic word of God.

This contrast plays a historical and theological role in the transition to monarchy. Historically, it explains a significant shift of power to come among various priestly families. Eli's family, which is thought to have descended from the Levites, is later replaced by Zadok's, an Aaronite family, during the rule of Solomon. The prophecy in 2:30–33 is fulfilled when Solomon bans Abiathar from the priesthood for supporting his rival (1 Kings 2:26–27). Behind the political intrigues and power struggles, the author of Samuel points to this moral and religious failure as the real reason for the decline of Eli's dynasty. This in return legitimises the leadership of Samuel, who, although he does not replace the priestly order, becomes the kingmaker.

Theologically it sets the scene for one of the most important questions of the time—the relationship between God's promise of an everlasting ministry/dynasty (2:30) and the failure of that ministry/dynasty to be faithful to God (3:13). This question will become a burning issue for Samuel himself, Saul, David and the future history of God's people.

2 The paradox of losing and winning

1 Samuel 4:1–11; 5:1–11; 6:1–15, 19–21

Many scholars see chapters 4—6 as a coherent distinctive narrative, perhaps one of the oldest parts of the book, portraying the ongoing struggle between Israel and the Philistines as found in the book of Judges. Nevertheless, the narrative has been incorporated within the broader historical and theological structure of Samuel. So, the judgement on Eli's children (2:34) finds fulfilment in this cycle of defeat and victory: it is implicitly acknowledged as the sole reason for the unexpected and devastating failure of Israel in chapter 4. The use of exodus imagery in the mouth of the fearful Philistines, while the Israelites lose seven times more troops than they had lost when the ark of God was *not* among them (4:2–3, 10), turns the whole defeat into a tragedy, an exodus in reverse.

However, the defeat is set, paradoxically, against a continuing portrayal of God as a sovereign king, a key theological concept in the events to come. It is in the book of Samuel that the title 'Lord of hosts' is encountered for the first time (1:3). The phrase could refer to the multitude of angels, creation or armies and is linked with royal imagery in the Psalms (see Psalm 24:10). Also, the ark of the covenant is brought into the battle as a royal throne on which 'the Lord of hosts… is enthroned on the cherubim' (4:4). The humiliation of a rival god, Dagon, followed by plagues (ch. 5), is used to point to the unfailing and unlimited power of the Lord king, who also rules his enemies.

It is interesting to note that the Lord is portrayed as acting independently, without the need of any human agent whether as a spokesman, leader or warrior—in contrast to other deliverance accounts (for example, the stories of the exodus, the entrance to the promise land or the exploits of the judges). Even the cart that holds the ark is divinely guided home (6:8–13).

This portrayal of God as self-sufficient and sovereign king is given as a preparatory context for the coming question of whether monarchy is is the appropriate solution to military threats. However, the author does not give us a naive answer. He also informs us of Israel's defeat, a condition that seems to have continued even after the return of the ark. This paradox of defeat and victory will play for and against the arguments of the chapters to come.

3 The need for repentance

1 Samuel 7

Chapter 7 addresses the paradox of the sovereignty of God and the continual invasions of the Philistines, which seem to have continued for 20 years. Religious renewal is set as the condition for participation in the victory and the kingship of God. This religious renewal is expressed in repentance and the refusal of idolatry. While it acknowledges the Lord's unique place within the community (v. 4), it also creates a sense of vulnerability and humility (v. 8), which was lacking from the description of the battles in chapter 4. So, the belief that victory is guaranteed simply by possession of the Lord's ark (4:3) gives way to supplication and intercession. In return, the lack of God's intervention on behalf of his people is reversed. The powerful deeds of the exodus, hinted at but never fulfilled in chapter 4, are now expressed in God's thunder (v. 10), an image commonly used in the Ancient Near East to describe divine beings as warriors. The author points at this reversal of outcome by using word play: the defeat at Ebenezer (4:1) is echoed by the stone that now commemorates God's help, also called Ebenezer (7:12).

The theme of repentance is described in emphatic language and becomes the model to be followed throughout the book of Samuel. The same confession, 'I/we have sinned against the Lord', appears at key moments in the life of Saul (1 Samuel 15:24) and David (2 Samuel 12:13). Their attitude to their failures and the nature of their repentance will dictate the outcome of their kingship. This will become an important message for the prophets when they address similar conditions in the decades to come (Hosea 14:1–2; Joel 2:12–13; Jeremiah 18:1–11).

In the wider context of the book, God's direct intervention is used to anticipate the argument that repentance, not a king, is required to save the people from defeat. This is emphasised by showing the extent of territory and peace that were recovered during Samuel's lifetime, something that was never achieved by Saul, the first king.

In our personal context, the theme of repentance in relation to the saving power of God reminds us to be cautious of any aspect of theology or symbolism that takes God's intervention for granted. Like the Israelites, we might bring the 'Lord's ark' into our 'battles', but without repenting and turning back to the Lord we might never experience his saving power.

4 The need for a king

1 Samuel 8

The events in chapter 8 take place after a long period of time, but they continue to address the question of whether a theocracy, as described in chapter 7, is adequate in the face of military threats. As in the case of Eli's sons, the corruption of the next generation's leaders becomes the Achilles' heel of theocracy. However, behind the social, economic and political risk of the proposed monarchy, the author draws attention to a deeper theological problem—that of replacing God's kingship. The demand for monarchy is described in verses 7–8 as following in the footsteps of idolatry; as a result, the call for divine help will not be answered (v. 18)—a direct contrast to chapter 7.

It is perplexing to see God give final permission for monarchy, despite the heavy note of condemnation. This has given rise to many opinions of how Israel's monarchy is evaluated throughout the biblical text, which sometimes accepts it as a neutral political progression (see, for example, Deuteronomy 17:14–20). For some scholars, the condemnation is more to do with Israel's desire to emulate the social order of 'the other nations' (vv. 5, 20) than with the institution of monarchy *per se*. They see Saul's failed kingship as being fuelled simply by the need for a military victory, while David's dynasty shows the Lord's blessing. Others see the narrative as reflecting the work of various editors, some of whom focus on the kings who brought positive religious reforms (for example, David and Josiah), while others understand monarchy as being ultimately responsible for the exile of the entire nation. However, we should be careful not to offer simplistic solutions that try to explain away the theological tension created by monarchy. There is no reason to deny the existence of opposing theological views among the contemporaries of Samuel; in the same way, today, we find among ourselves a range of theo-political views. The book of Judges, too, hints at this old conundrum (Judges 8:22–23; 21:25).

The complexity of the story carries a wide range of implications concerning the monopoly of power in our personal lives, ecclesiastical set-ups and our society. It challenges us to consider the deeper theological questions behind the socio-economic aims of any establishment. It points to the danger and the dilemma of restructuring societies without taking into account God's role, despite the security that they seem to provide.

5 Rehabilitation of monarchy

1 Samuel 9:1–2, 15–17; 10:1, 9–27; 12:13–24

Chapters 9—12 give us, in a series of narratives, the confirmation of the new king, Saul, and the rehabilitation of the institution of monarchy within the theological frame of God's covenant with his people. There is a series of tensions between these chapters and chapter 8, which has led some scholars to interpret them as coming from different sources, but, as Robert Polzin points out, these tensions could be literary tools employed by the author to shape and guide the reader's perspective (*Samuel and the Deuteronomist*, p. 89). For example, Samuel is an important, well-established political leader in chapter 8, but in chapter 9 he is an almost unknown fortune teller for whom Saul has to search hard to get advice over a mundane issue. The author seems to be suppressing the reader's previous knowledge about Samuel in order to link the quest for a king with the precarious search for the true prophet who can proclaim God's verdict—a relationship that will play a significant role during the period of monarchy.

Saul's kingship is confirmed by a direct word from God, an ecstatic experience of God's Spirit, a public casting of lots and a military victory. In light of these events, it would be difficult to dismiss the Lord's blessing on Saul's kingship, as some commentators have done. In fact, in the narrative, those who previously doubted his kingship are now described by the author as 'worthless' people (10:27). The softening of language towards the king is even more noticeable in God's own words (9:16), which seem distant from the absolutism expressed in chapter 7. Whether this softening is linked with the fact that here Saul is described only as a leader (*ngid*), and not a king (*melek*), is widely debated among scholars.

The criticism of monarchy is resumed in chapters 10 and 12, with slight adjustments, the most striking of which is the fact that God reconfirms his covenant commitment to his people, despite their sins (12:14, 20–22). The people's confession does not cancel the institution of monarchy but, rather, purifies it and incorporates it within God's covenant. In this way the danger of monarchy is redefined: the risk no longer lies in the idolatrous act of replacing God's kingship but in the king's potential failure to follow God's law. The king is placed not above God's law or equal to it, but underneath it, subject to the same blessings and curses as the rest of the community.

6 The rejection of Saul (I)

1 Samuel 13:1–15

The Hebrew text of the book of Samuel, as represented in the Masoretic text, contains a considerable number of textual difficulties throughout. There are many cryptic words or phrases that perplex scholars even today. These difficulties are sometimes considered to be scribal errors or archaic forms that do not comply with our knowledge of ancient Hebrew and, on occasions, give us a reading different from the one found in other ancient manuscripts, such as the Septuagint. The first verse of chapter 13 is one of the most well-known of these difficulties. The Hebrew text, 'a son of a year… and for two years he ruled…', gives the impression that Saul was only one year old when he became a king and ruled until he was three years old. This obviously contradicts the content of the narrative.

Scholars who try to maintain the Masoretic wording interpret the 'one year' as meaning 'a certain age', as if the author did not know the exact age of Saul. They also see the length of 'two years' as representing the short period during which Saul counted as a king before God (13:13–14), although, from a human perspective, his rule was longer than that. Other scholars, who see this verse as a scribal error, tend to amend it in different ways, based on other ancient sources. Sometimes the length of Saul's reign is amended to 40 years, in accordance with Acts 13:21 and Josephus' *Antiquities*. His age at his accession is either left empty, in accordance with a technique found in the Babylonian Chronicles when the author was not aware of a king's age, or given as 30, based on some manuscripts of the Septuagint.

Although these details might seem irrelevant to readers today, the nature of the textual problems found in general in the book of Samuel cautions us to pay closer attention to the whole range of textual sources and linguistic arguments before making a particular word or phrase key to our theological discussions or sermons.

Guidelines

As we reflect on the first 13 chapters of 1 Samuel, we look back at the psalm of Hannah in 2:1–10. This anticipates some key theological themes addressed in the chapters that we have covered. The theme of God's power, his willingness to intervene, to uproot and reverse social orders, and to bring deliverance and judgement, permeates the entire book of Samuel. The divine power that Hannah praises is joyful and terrifying. It brings deliverance to the humble, but judgement and humiliation to those who stand against it. As the story of Eli's sons, Samuel's sons and Saul's failed kingship has shown us, the object of that humiliation is not just the enemy. The social establishment of priesthood, judges and kingship is overturned when it deviates from God's rule. However, in the middle of this uprooting the Lord also brings the hope of starting a new thing. The young Samuel is raised as the priestly family declines, Saul is given as king despite the people's rejection of the Lord's power, and a new king according to the Lord's heart is on the way to replace a disobedient Saul.

Therefore, as we read Hannah's prayer, we might take some time in silence to reflect on the following questions:

- Who holds the monopoly on power in our lives?
- Where does our confidence rest in times of crisis?
- Are there any areas in our lives where we are not allowing God to rule?
- Is there an aspect of our lives that the Lord needs to uproot in order to start afresh?

1 The rejection of Saul (2)

1 Samuel 15

The story of Saul's rejection as king is similar to the one in chapter 13, where his dynasty is also rejected. Both accounts deal with a religious offence taking place at Gilgal and leading to a confrontation with Samuel. The object of Saul's offence in chapter 15 is the extent to which he has carried out 'the ban', which was the practice of dedicating the enemy by killing them and destroying all their possessions as a sacrifice to the deity. It is found in both biblical and extrabiblical materials (Deuteronomy 13:17; Joshua 6:17; ANET, 320).

The concept of the ban poses moral difficulties for us, which can skew our evaluation of Saul's action. Should his failure to carry out a 'religious atrocity' be considered worthy of praise rather than condemnation? Was Saul being more reasonable, more merciful and more politically astute than Samuel and, ultimately, God? These are valid questions that need to be considered within the broader context of the Old Testament.

However, within the theological frame of the author, the question is not about the validity of such actions. Saul himself later acted in a similar way against the city of Nob even without divine sanction (1 Samuel 22:19). For the author, the main reason for his failure was an attempt to put his role as monarch above the role of Samuel, the prophet (in chapter 13), and of God's commandments (in chapter 15)—two key elements that served in the previous chapters to accommodate the institution of monarchy.

Saul's repentance falls short of the emphatic language used to describe the repentance of the people at Mizpah (ch. 7). His confession, 'I have sinned', comes only after a long series of failed attempts to justify his actions, and its sincerity is subtly called into question as he continues to be portrayed as someone who is afraid of losing popularity (v. 30), even after accepting that this was the very reason for his sin (v. 24).

Verse 29 is perplexing and has given rise to differing interpretations. While this verse categorically states that God does not change his mind when giving a verdict, we are also told that God did change his mind about making Saul king (vv. 11, 35). Some scholars interpret verse 29 as a later editorial comment, inserted to clarify the impossibility of the return of Saul's dynasty. Others see it as the sign of an ongoing theological paradox involving God's eternal promises or decrees and the possibility of change because of human disobedience and repentance.

2 The rise of David

1 Samuel 16

The events that lead to Saul's rejection are regarded by some as an attempt by Samuel to trick a political opponent who has refused to be his puppet. However, the author seems to anticipate this criticism by pointing to the Lord himself as the one who rejects Saul, puts an end to Samuel's mourning and initiates the quest for another king.

Saul's rejection and replacement are pointedly contrasted with David's anointing and physical appearance and the activity of God's Spirit. His physical attributes become the central focus in this chapter. The same physical qualities that were praised in Saul's election (9:2; 10:23–24) are now dismissed in the assessment of Eliab, David's brother (16:6–7). Samuel's previous optimism and confidence in Saul's election are also now contrasted with his inability to see what God sees. However, despite the Lord's warning, David is still introduced with the same praise of his physical appearance (v. 12). Whether this description is meant positively or ironically is ambiguous. On one hand, the same expression, 'ruddy and handsome', is used in 17:42 to express Goliath's derision of David and his ability to fight. On the other, the theme of beauty crops up again when Absalom is introduced as an attractive contender for the throne (2 Samuel 14:25–26).

God's spirit comes upon David and immediately departs from Saul, to be replaced by a tormenting spirit (vv. 13–14). Saul's condition is perplexing to us, for two reasons. First, it is difficult to say whether the 'evil spirit' is a metaphor for depression, which is lifted by pleasant music, or an actual demonic possession. Second, the idea that the Lord is behind the sending of an evil spirit is challenging. Some scholars have argued, from a linguistic perspective, that the expression does not refer to a demonic being, but to the same spirit of the Lord, who, in this case, brings evil or judgement. However, even an understanding of a demonic being can be accommodated within the theological framework that no power, even an evil power, can act independently from God's rule. As we see in 1 Kings 22:19–23, all spirits are in his service: God is the ultimate source, the one who 'kills and brings to life… brings down to Sheol and raises up' (1 Samuel 2:6).

3 David and Goliath

1 Samuel 17

Following the pattern of Saul's accession to kingship, David's anointing is followed by an experience of the Lord's spirit (16:13), which culminates here in a military battle. The need for deliverance from the Philistines was a key element in the people's plea for a king, despite the fact that it resulted in a rejection of God's kingship. Therefore, there is an expectation that a victory by David, as the king 'after God's own heart' (13:14), should also bring a theological restoration between God's role and that of the king. There is no surprise, then, that beneath the narrative of an impossible victory there are theological hints of past episodes.

David's reply to Goliath provides the key to this theological restoration. First, the Lord, and not the king, is described as being at the heart of Israel's fate (v. 45; compare v. 8). Second, it is the 'Lord of hosts' who ultimately provides the victory, beyond the military power. Third, the purpose of this victory is to bring glory and expand the Lord's prestige. By bringing the theological implication of God's rule and power to the heart of a crisis, David does what the people forgot to do when asking for a king in the face of a similar threat, and what Saul failed to do when disobeying the Lord's commandments before and after his battles. The model provided here by David becomes, for the author, the prototype of a godly king.

From a textual perspective, the story of David and Goliath contains many points of tension. For example, although David has been described in chapter 16 as an important servant of Saul, here Saul does not seem to know him at all. The brothers, too, seem unaware of David's anointing. David is said to bring Goliath's head to Jerusalem, although Jerusalem was still not part of Israel's territory, and Goliath is reported elsewhere as having been killed by Elhanan (2 Samuel 21:19). There have been many reasonable attempts to harmonise these tensions, but the overall opinion among scholars is that chapter 17 comes from a separate tradition, introducing David's claim to kingship from a military perspective. According to Robert Alter, the author incorporates the different traditions on purpose to illustrate David's complex personality as both a gentle spirit and a fearless warrior—two contrasting personas that will shape his life.

4 David and Saul

1 Samuel 18:1–16, 20–22; 19:8–24

The rest of the book of Samuel is concerned with the struggle between David and Saul. In comparison to the spectacular battle against Goliath, inner conflicts are now shown in more depth and length. Also, divine intervention is more sporadic but is intertwined with the complexity of human politics. The author's concern is to legitimise David's claim to the throne before Saul's family, his loyal servants and the rest of the people. All of these social classes are described by the author as 'loving' David (18:1, 16, 20, 22). In contrast to them, however, stands Saul, who not only fears David (18:12) but also plots to assassinate or capture him in four separate episodes in chapter 19. Saul's deteriorating power reaches its lowest point in 19:20–24, where the same ecstatic experience that enabled him to become king (10:9–12) now strips him of all self-control.

David's relationship with Jonathan takes centre stage. As the legitimate successor to Saul, Jonathan enjoyed a high degree of loyalty among the army and the people. This is hinted at in 1 Samuel 14, where the people support him at the cost of standing against Saul. Therefore, the love for David that the author ascribes to Jonathan has immense political implications for David's claim to the throne.

The emphatic language used has raised many comments about the nature of the relationship between David and Jonathan. Those who emphasise the emotional (20:17) or even the erotic side (2 Samuel 1:26) often use this passage to support the idea of a homosexual relationship. However, the sexual nature of the relationship, in my opinion, is an interpretation imposed upon the text from a reader's perspective. As it stands within the wider context of the book, the expression of love towards David is used by the author to show political patronage. In fact, it is Saul who is first said to have loved David (16:21), and the same word for 'love' is used to describe people's loyalty towards him (18:16). In 1 Kings 5:1 (translated as 'friend'), it refers to a diplomatic relationship between Hiram and David. Even when the word 'love' is used to describe his wife's feelings (18:28), it is still in the context of a political struggle between Saul and David. For the author, the transfer of political power is the underlying issue, symbolised by the handing over of Jonathan's clothes to David (18:4).

5 David spares Saul

1 Samuel 26

David's escape in chapter 19 is followed by a series of attempts by Saul to capture him. This military quest reaches a climax when the two contenders confront each other face to face. Chapters 24 and 26 refer to this encounter. Based on the degree of similarity, it is possible that the two accounts describe the same historical event from different perspectives. Interestingly, the author separates the two accounts with chapter 25, which serves as a commentary on David's reasons for not taking revenge against Saul.

Abigail's speech in 1 Samuel 25:26–31 provides the heart of the argument for David to follow a policy of appeasal towards his political opponents. Beyond the theological reasoning, she hints at the benefits of stability, acceptance and the legitimacy of David's rule, if he is to show mercy. The author has already indicated his approval of this policy by introducing Abigail as an intelligent and wise woman (25:3, 33), and this is followed by a change of heart from David, who has been preparing for revenge against Nabal (25:13, 21–22, 33).

The theological aspect of the same policy of appeasal is sharpened in chapter 26. Abigail's argument in favour of leaving revenge to the Lord and preserving David's innocence is now reused by David himself. In contrast, though, his argument does not focus on the political benefits for his future kingdom; rather, it stems from a desire to honour God's choice of Saul as his anointed. The shift of perspective from political benefits to theological implications reminds us once again, as in the story of Goliath, how the figure of David encourages us to consider the role of God at the heart of a crisis. David's argument does not make the monarch unaccountable for any other human responsibilities (despite the way the text may have been misused through the centuries); rather, it revives a focus on God's direct intervention in the institution of monarchy.

At a personal level, this account challenges us to leave revenge in God's hands and, as in Romans 12:17–21, reminds us to overcome evil with good. However, in a socio-political context it raises many challenging questions about God's will in relation to his anointing, our responsibilities and abusive powers. What determines whether an authority, even an abusive one like that of Saul, is still ordained by God? Does David's example give support in such cases only to a peaceful resistance?

6 Saul's death

1 Samuel 28:3–19; 30:1–20; 31:1–6

The final days of Saul are set in direct contrast to David's initiation into kingship. So, both Saul and David experience distress from a military threat (28:5; 30:4), but whereas Saul fails to gain the Lord's counsel (28:6), David is said to find strength in the Lord (30:6). Saul's attempt to attain an answer from the Lord through necromancy is contrasted with David's use of the priest and ephod. Saul's actions are described in tragic and desperate terms as he turns against his own laws and beliefs. There is an element of ridicule here, as he tries to assure the medium of her safety by swearing on the 'Lord as he lives' even while he is turning to the dead to enquire about his own safety (28:10–11). His anguish is intensified by an excessive use of verbs that refer to asking. So Saul (or the medium on his behalf) inquires (v. 6), seeks out (v. 7), consults (v. 8), brings up (v. 11) and summons (v. 15), only to be told what he already knows—that he has been condemned by God for his failure against Amalek (28:18; see ch. 15). On the other hand, David receives divine guidance and victory: he defeats Amalek, the cause of Saul's downfall—although the issue of the destruction of spoils of war is not considered any more (30:20).

The issue of necromancy has perplexed many Jewish and Christian interpreters through the centuries. As early as the fourth century AD,

Origen and Eustathius debated whether the appearance of Samuel's ghost was theologically possible or was merely demonic. The text, however, is not concerned with metaphysical discussions. The practice was clearly forbidden in ancient Israel (Deuteronomy 18:10–11; Leviticus 19:31; 20:6), but here it is used to point to Saul's sinful deterioration. In 1 Samuel 15:23, his rebellion and stubbornness were considered as sinful as divination and idolatry—offences that now find their ultimate expression.

Saul is the most tragic figure in the first book of Samuel. He is a failed leader who, for the reason of mere disobedience, slides away from the Lord's favour, standing against God's anointed one, slaughtering the Lord's priests and finally turning against God and losing himself. For the author, Saul's failure to obey becomes the underlying reason for the failure of the kingdom. Yet it opens the way for the coming of a king 'after God's own heart', a theme that will also inspire messianic hopes after the exile.

Guidelines

Many of David's psalms can be related to the threats and political intrigues described in the book of Samuel. They provide a window into David's anguish, fears, hope and faith, which not only helps us to understand the man behind the story but also sets a model for us to follow. Psalm 57 is a personal lament of David, attributed to the time when he escaped from Saul and hid in a cave (1 Samuel 22 or 24). We could use this psalm as a basis for reflection.

Read Psalm 57, paying attention to the description of David's distress. Try to recall, visualise or write down episodes from the book of Samuel that fit such descriptions. Reflect silently for a few minutes. Then read the psalm again. This time, try to recall past or present episodes from your own life that could echo David's distress. Reflect silently for a few minutes.

Read the psalm slowly once more, paying attention to the description of God's intervention. Reflect silently for a few minutes. Finally, write a short prayer bringing together your current difficulties with the hope of God's intervention.

FURTHER READING

David Tsumura, *The First Book of Samuel* (New International Commentary on the Old Testament), Eerdmans, 2006.

Walter Brueggemann, *First and Second Samuel* (Interpretation Bible Commentaries), John Knox Press, 1990.

Ralph Klein, *1 Samuel* (Word Biblical Commentary), Nelson, 1989.

Robert Polzin, *Samuel and the Deuteronomist: A literary study of the Deuteronomic History*, Indiana University Press, 1993.

Acts 17—28

This section of Acts will take us from Athens to Rome, from Paul as a free man to Paul as a prisoner, from engaging with pagans to engaging with Jews. Throughout, Luke focuses our attention on God and his work in the world, for Acts is a book about God and what God is doing. Luke is concerned to show how the gospel message of Jesus has an impact in different situations. It isn't only when Paul is out in the marketplace of Athens that the gospel is making an impact—it's also when Paul the prisoner stands before rulers and tells his story of meeting the exalted Jesus.

Look for God's activity throughout this section of Acts, and keep asking what God is doing section by section in the story. Look for the gospel message, what it is and how it is communicated, and look for the way God guards and protects his people, notably Paul, through suffering and pressure.

A particular feature of Acts 17—19 is that we see Paul planting churches in major cities. He spends at least 18 months in Corinth and two years in Ephesus, and through his ministry in those places the hinterland of the cities is touched, notably in Ephesus, where (with pardonable hyperbole) Luke writes that the whole province of Asia heard the message (Acts 19:10). In both cities, Paul faces significant and serious opposition: the planting of churches is not an easy task. Paul finds God's power at work in them both, and he needs to learn to stand off and watch what God does, for God acts through people who are not gospel people to protect and guard those who are. God is truly great, and the exalted Jesus, whom Paul met on the Damascus road, reigns from heaven.

1 Introducing God to the Athenians

Acts 17:16–34

Mars Hill is a mound just below the Parthenon in Athens; here Paul met with the Areopagus, the city's supreme council (v. 22). The Areopagus assessed proposals to build temples for new gods being introduced to Athens. For the proposal to be accepted, the proposer had to show that there was evidence of the god's activity and that there were sufficient funds available to build the temple, provide for priests and endow an annual feast day.

So after Paul's debates in the marketplace, they say, using legal technical terms, 'We have a legal right to judge this new teaching that is being spoken by you, and so we wish to make a judgement on what you claim these things are' (vv. 19–20, my translation). The question is polite, because someone who proposed the introduction of a new god would be wealthy and so would be treated with respect.

Paul's response is devastating, as he replies using scripture and Greco-Roman writers. No temple needs to be created for the one true God, because he is the creator of all things and does not inhabit handmade temples (v. 24). No priests and other staff are required for the temple, and no designated feast day, for God does not need such things; instead, he generously gives people life and much else (v. 25). No statue is necessary to bring God near (v. 29), for God is near to all (v. 27), as the Greek poet Epimenides says (quoted, v. 28). The true God does not require introduction in Athens, for he is already known as 'an unknown god' (v. 23). Thus, people need to repent—to change their minds and reorientate their lives around the true God—and the proof of all this is Jesus' resurrection (vv. 30–31).

Paul turns the tables on the Areopagus: their request for information to make a judgement about Jesus is utterly wrong-headed, for Jesus is the one who judges them. They must answer to the true God, rather than God answering to them. Human arrogance has not changed since Paul's day: people still put themselves at the centre of the universe and decide whether God known in Jesus will fit into their view. The Areopagus speech shows the errors of this approach and summons people to a better way.

2 It's God's work, and God will do it

Acts 18:1–17

Corinth was a multicultural port city, with visitors and permanent residents from all around the Mediterranean. We can date Paul's visit, because a person was only the proconsul (senior Roman officer) of any place for a year—and we know that Gallio was proconsul of Achaia, the Roman province, when Paul was in Corinth (v. 12). This places Paul's 18-month visit to Corinth (v. 11) in AD50–52. As Paul works to establish a believing community in the city, he faces two major challenges, both stemming from some of the Jewish population.

First, Paul is rejected by the majority of the synagogue (v. 6)—a synagogue which was probably large, swelled by Jewish people who had been thrown out of Rome after Emperor Claudius' decree (v. 2). The rejecters are not the only Jews in Corinth, though, for some believe, including one of the synagogue officials, Crispus (v. 8). God is still at work, and Titius Justus, a 'godfearer' (a Gentile who was very sympathetic to Judaism but had not been circumcised), provides a base in which Paul's new congregation can meet (v. 7). Here the Lord (probably Jesus) makes a key promise to Paul, of his presence with and protection of Paul. But notice: it is not that Paul won't be attacked but that 'no one will lay a hand on you *with the result that you are harmed*' (vv. 9–10, my translation and my emphasis). Jesus will stand by Paul in suffering, not protect him from suffering for the gospel—and the very next story shows God's protection at work.

Second, the synagogue Jews haul Paul before proconsul Gallio, seeking to have Paul judged for crimes against 'the law' (vv. 12–13), although *which law*, Luke does not say. Gallio thinks it is the Jewish law and thus rejects their charges (v. 15). Most strikingly, as Paul is just about to open his mouth, Gallio intervenes (v. 14). In fact, Paul is completely inactive and silent in Luke's story of the 'trial' before Gallio: the only two mentions of him are that the synagogue Jews bring him to Gallio and that he fails to speak. God is fulfilling his promise that Paul will not be harmed in the middle of this attack on him by the synagogue Jews, and Paul does not even need to say a word for this to happen.

3 The baptiser connection in Ephesus

Acts 18:24—19:10

From Corinth, Paul travels to Jerusalem (18:22) before returning to Asia Minor (western Turkey). Luke now focuses on Ephesus, the provincial capital. Paul will spend a substantial time—over two years—in Ephesus, as in Corinth, planting and establishing a church (19:8, 10). Ephesus was a big city of over 300,000 in the first century and became a strategic centre for people throughout the province to hear the gospel (19:10). The church in Colosse, about 175km/109 miles up the valley of the river Lycus from Ephesus, was planted by Epaphras, a Colossian native who met Paul, probably in Ephesus, and became his 'fellow worker' (Colossians 1:7; 4:12–13).

Before Paul arrives, we meet Apollos, a powerful speaker who knows about Jesus, but only partially. Hence, Paul's associates Priscilla and Aquila (whom Paul met in Corinth, 18:2–3) spend time teaching Apollos and filling the gaps in his understanding (18:26). Unusually for the ancient world, Priscilla is named first in Luke's account, which may suggest that she took the lead in teaching Apollos. Their approach is not to criticise Apollos' inadequate knowledge publicly but to complete it privately. Apollos' knowledge stems from his association with John the baptiser, whose mission was to prepare the way for Jesus (Luke 3:15–17), so presumably what Priscilla and Aquila do is to show how Jesus completed John's prophecies about him—in other words, that Jesus was the Jewish Messiah (18:28).

The connection with John the baptiser continues in the next story, for Paul himself encounters a dozen of John's followers (19:1, 3, 7). They may well have been travelling missionaries for the baptiser's message, as Paul and his co-workers were for the gospel of Jesus. Paul asks them to assess themselves using a crucial diagnostic question: 'Did you receive the Holy Spirit when you became believers?' (19:2). For Paul and other New Testament writers, *the* mark of a true believer is their experience of the Spirit (see, for example, Romans 8:9). The fact that he asks this question implies that people must themselves know whether or not the Spirit is in their lives. In Galatians 3:2 and 5 he asks a similar question, suggesting that the experience of the Spirit's varied gifts marks out true believers. This raises the question of whether some professing Christians today are like these twelve believers—knowing part of the story but not experiencing the Spirit, who brings the reality of Christ into human lives.

4 Evil in Ephesus

Acts 19:11–41

As in Corinth (18:4–6), so in Ephesus: Paul's proclamation of the gospel message divides the synagogue, and some Jews begin to follow Jesus and meet regularly with Paul. Furthermore, God adds his testimony to Paul's by healing and delivering people from spiritual oppression (19:11–12). It all looks good—but then spiritual conflict takes centre stage for the rest of Paul's time in Ephesus.

The Jewish exorcists unwisely attempt to deliver people by second- or third-hand use of Jesus' name (vv. 13–14). Exorcists often used a powerful name in a spell or exorcism, expecting the name itself to be effective—and the name of Jesus is certainly powerful (see, for example, 3:6–8). However, the crucial thing is not the name itself but the relationship with Jesus to which it points—and Paul knows Jesus in experience but the Jewish exorcists do not (v. 15). In consequence, the evil spirit enables the man to beat up the exorcists (v. 16). From this rather comical story, honour and glory comes to Jesus, for people realise that people who know Jesus have greater power than the evil spirits—and new believers see that they cannot continue their former magical practices while following Jesus (vv. 18–19).

Paul's evangelism also damages the trade of those who make silver shrines of the city's patron goddess, Artemis (vv. 24–26). Her massive temple, the Artemision, dominated the city skyline. It was a place of sacrifice and worship: the Ephesians believed that Artemis' statue had fallen from heaven (see v. 35). The city's main bank was also based there, and it was the focus for a large sex trade. Festivals of Artemis punctuated the annual calendar. The cult of Artemis overshadowed the entire culture of the city: to be disloyal to her was to be disloyal to Ephesus. Therefore, to cause economic problems for Artemis' traders, as Paul does, is to insult the goddess (v. 27), and a riot ensues (vv. 28–34).

Here is another case, as in Corinth (18:14), where doing nothing is the right thing to do. Paul's friends persuade him to stay away from the riot (vv. 30–31), and the town clerk's wise words prevent further problems (vv. 35–40). God works through this non-believer's words, which, unknown to him, fulfil Jesus' promise that Paul will not be harmed (18:10).

5 Paul the pastor

Acts 20:7–38

Until now, Luke's Paul has been an action man—a church planter and defender of the Christian faith. Now the scene changes and we get glimpses of Paul the pastor, who cares deeply for his churches—the Paul of his letters. Paul models pastoral care in Troas, in teaching the church about following Jesus (vv. 7, 11), and in his compassionate prayer for Eutychus. This young man, remarkably, revives when Paul falls on him after the manner of Elijah with another dead boy (vv. 8–10; see 1 Kings 17:17–24; Acts 9:36–42). Paul the pastor celebrates the Lord's supper there too (v. 11).

Paul loves the Ephesian Christians deeply but he wants to be in Jerusalem for Pentecost (v. 16), so he cannot divert to Ephesus. Instead, he sends for the leaders of the Ephesian church to meet him at Miletus (v. 17), the port where Paul's ship has docked. Paul charges these leaders to follow his example, echoing Jesus' 'farewell speech' (Luke 22:14–38). Jesus spoke of facing future suffering, both his own (22:15, 28, 37) and his followers' (vv. 31–32). Jesus called his disciples to sit loose to money and possessions and to trust God to provide (22:35). He modelled servant leadership and contrasted the self-seeking leadership of Gentile rulers with the leadership style he wanted (22:24–30). All this was rooted in Jesus' words and actions with bread and wine, highlighting the powerful effects of his death (22:19–20).

Similarly, here, Paul highlights the importance of faithful leadership that flows from a servant heart. Like Jesus, Paul is ready to suffer for the truth (Acts 20:22–24), and the elders, too, will meet threats (vv. 29–30). Paul is generous with money and possessions, in order to help needy believers (vv. 33–34), and the elders are to behave in the same way (v. 35). Paul points to his own faithful leadership, with readiness for costly service of the Lord and others at its centre (vv. 18–21, 26–27), and calls the elders to do the same (vv. 28–31). At the centre of Paul's pastoring is Jesus, who gave his blood (v. 28), his life laid down in death, and nothing Paul suffers compares with that. It is Jesus' love for the church, the community that God purchased (v. 28, 'obtained' in NRSV) at enormous cost, which drives and enables Paul to be a pastor, and will similarly equip and empower the elders.

6 Another gospel riot, in Jerusalem

Acts 21:17–36

Paul was no stranger to riots (19:29)! Jewish opposition to Paul and his gospel is at the root of the one in Jerusalem. At an earlier Jerusalem meeting, the elders, including Paul and Peter, had agreed that Gentiles were welcome as believers without being circumcised as Jews or keeping Jewish laws (v. 25; 15:19–20). So what of the Jewish believers? They were free to observe Jewish laws and traditions, but now within faith in Jesus and in fellowship with Gentile believers. Some people thought that Paul rejected this freedom, telling Jews not to circumcise their sons or keep the Jewish law (v. 21)—which was untrue. The leaders of the thriving Jewish believing communities (v. 20) want to demonstrate fellowship with Paul, so they ask him to take a Jewish vow along with others (vv. 23–24). Paul's missional approach includes the principle that 'to those under the [Jewish] law I became like one under the law… so as to win those under the law' (1 Corinthians 9:20), so he is willing to take the vow.

Things go wrong because some Jews (probably not believers) who have followed Paul from Asia stir up the crowds by wrongly accusing Paul of taking the Gentile Trophimus into a part of the temple reserved for Jews (vv. 27–29). Such Gentiles would defile the temple. Archaeologists have found a sign from this point in the temple which warns any Gentile who passes it that they will be responsible for their certain death.

The ensuing riot shows how quickly the crowd could be stirred up emotionally by this claim: it went to the heart of the very high regard in which the Jewish people held the temple and its holiness, as well as the law. It is striking to see the parallel with the earlier accusations against Stephen, claiming that he had attacked the law and the temple (6:13–14). Nuances and subtleties of theology are not heard when emotions are stirred, and Paul's life is in real danger (v. 31a).

Once again God keeps his promise of guarding Paul's safety (18:10). Once again, the Romans protect Paul: the tribune of the Fortress of Antonia, which overshadowed one corner of the temple courts, sends soldiers in, and they grab Paul and carry him to safety on the fortress steps (vv. 32–35). This must have been a scary experience; yet God did not abandon Paul and kept his word of protection.

Guidelines

The exalted Lord Jesus is determined that the gospel message will reach into the Gentile world, and invites his people to share that determination. This poses serious questions to our churches today, asking us whether we share these priorities or whether we have settled into 'maintenance' mode and pushed mission to the periphery of our lives, individually and collectively.

God's promise to keep Paul safe even through suffering and pressure (18:10) dominates this section of Acts, and it is a promise given to one who shares the Lord's commitment to his mission. God does not write Paul a blank cheque: God will not keep Paul safe whatever Paul does; rather, God will sustain and uphold Paul and will protect him from being crushed as he walks in the path to which Jesus calls him. It is the path of truth and suffering, which belong closely together in the mission of God.

This poses a second question (and a key diagnostic one) to our churches today: are we so similar to our culture and society that we do not suffer for the gospel? If our church life and proclamation are not challenging our society's values, beliefs and ideology, the world has no reason to change—for we are just like the world around us.

It is worth reflecting positively on these two challenges. First, how am I, and how is my church, engaged in a mission that brings a different, godly perspective to bear on life today? Where does the gospel of Jesus challenge our society and its values, and how can my fellowship act as Jesus' agents in engaging with that society?

Second, where am I, and where is my Christian community, facing pressure or suffering for our stand for the gospel? It's possible, of course, to be an irritant to others for the wrong reasons; we need to ask where we are being an irritant like a piece of grit in a pearl, which produces something beautiful at the end of the process.

Talk with others in your fellowship about these questions, and reflect on how God calls and invites you, through Acts, to respond.

1 Paul's 'defence' in the temple

Acts 21:37—22:30

We left Paul in Roman hands, with crowds wanting his blood (21:35–36). Yet within a short time the crowd falls silent and listens carefully. Why? First, Paul, seemingly unfazed by the situation, asks the tribune's permission to speak to the people (v. 39). He motions for silence, which he surprisingly receives, and the silence deepens as they hear Aramaic (a close relative of Hebrew, 22:2), the crowd's mother-tongue. Here is Paul's chance to put things straight.

However, Paul offers no direct response to the claim that he has defiled the temple (21:28). Instead, he speaks about his own meeting with Jesus—far more important than defending himself. The heart of Paul's speech is his encounter with the exalted Jesus on the Damascus road (22:6–11). This is the second time (of three) that Luke tells this story (see also 9:1–9; 26:12–18), which signals its significance. Here, we see the story through Paul's eyes, and the focus is on the person whom Paul encountered. Paul asked about that person's identity and learnt that he was Jesus of Nazareth (v. 8). Paul then realised that the exalted Jesus was to be obeyed, so he asked about Jesus' purposes for him (v. 10). Paul was humbled, dependent on others to lead him (v. 11) and dependent on Jesus to guide him.

Guidance came through Ananias (vv. 12–16), who told him that he would be Jesus' witness 'to all the world' (v. 15, NRSV). Here is the first hint given to Paul that non-Jews would be able to join the believing community. The guidance was sharpened in Paul's vision in the temple (of all places!), where Jesus made explicit his call to Paul to speak to Gentiles (v. 21).

The crowd's predictable response is to call for Paul's death (vv. 22–23): their opposition comes because the implication of Jesus' universal rule is that all races are to be drawn into the circle of God's love, not the Jews only. Paul takes every opportunity to speak of Jesus to others, even at great danger to himself.

Paul is again under threat, and the tribune adopts standard Roman procedure—to learn the truth using torture (v. 24). Now Paul declares his Roman citizenship, as he did in Philippi (16:37–38): this will keep the door open for him to speak the gospel, for that is his priority.

2 The route to Rome

Acts 25:1–27

Paul spent a long time—two years or more (24:27)—in custody in Caesarea, after a first hearing that ended in stalemate. Lysias, who arrested Paul, was unavailable to testify (24:22), and Governor Felix was not disposed to free Paul without a bribe (24:26). The situation was manifestly unjust: Paul had done nothing wrong. Doubtless he had been praying and reflecting about what he might do. How could he respond to this injustice rightly and, more importantly, in a way that would commend the gospel?

The chance comes when the governor changes. Festus, the new postholder, wisely wants to meet the Jewish leaders quickly, to inform his governing, and they take this chance to accuse Paul (v. 2). They are in no doubt that Paul must die, and are secretly plotting to achieve their goal (v. 3), so how will God's promise of protection (18:10) be fulfilled here?

In God's providence, Festus declines to hear Paul's case in Jerusalem, keeping Paul safe for the present in Caesarea (vv. 4–5). When the Jewish authorities accuse Paul, he adopts a different strategy from before: he simply denies their accusations (v. 8). Then, when Festus proposes a hearing in Jerusalem, Paul appeals to the emperor (vv. 10–11). It was the right of a Roman citizen to have his case heard before the empire's supreme ruler, Caesar—but why does Paul want this to happen? There could be at least two reasons. First, Paul is now convinced that he will not get justice in Judea and wants the opportunity to be cleared so that he will be free to travel and carry out his apostolic ministry. We know from Romans 15:25–28 (written in Corinth, en route to Jerusalem) that Paul intended, after visiting Jerusalem, to go to Rome and then to Spain. Second, and more significantly, Paul has the Lord's promise that he will bear testimony in Rome (23:11)—and he sees his appeal as offering a chance to speak to the emperor, the ruler of the world, about the true world ruler, Jesus. The Paul who took every opportunity to speak with others about Jesus would be unlikely to miss *that* chance! The die is now cast, and Paul is on his way to Rome.

3 It's Jesus who speaks: Paul before Agrippa

Acts 26

Festus must write a trial brief to send with Paul to Rome (25:26–27), and he is confused, for he considers Paul undeserving of death (25:25). So Festus takes the opportunity of the visit of Agrippa, the part-Jewish client-ruler of the region, with his sister Bernice, to learn more. They have expertise in Jewish affairs (26:3), and may inform what Festus writes.

Paul's approach to Agrippa is similar to his approach to the temple crowds: he offers testimony about Jesus to persuade Agrippa to follow Jesus too (v. 29). In this third telling of his conversion, Paul again highlights the identity of the one who appeared to him. After a sketch of Paul's earlier life of Jewish zeal and his persecution of believers (vv. 4–11) comes the surprise for Agrippa, as Paul tells how he was changed by his encounter with the exalted Jesus, becoming a zealous advocate for the faith he once opposed (vv. 12–18). The new information here is that Jesus commissioned Paul *on the day of their first meeting* to go to the Gentiles (vv. 17–18). At the same time, Jesus promised Paul his protection (v. 17), a point reiterated at key points in Acts (notably 18:10; 23:11; 27:23–24).

Paul speaks with great confidence, and he does so because he is not really the one doing the proclamation; he is simply Jesus' advocate and voice. It is Jesus himself who proclaims light—the gospel—to both Jew and Gentile (v. 23b). The resurrection marks Jesus out for this distinctive role (v. 23a). He is now active in many times and places, with his witnesses, to communicate the gospel, open people's eyes and move wills to respond. These activities hint and signal that Jesus is more than human, for it takes God to communicate God and lead people to experience God. Although the Roman empire is powerful, its servants are called to recognise that Jesus is the world's true ruler: Jesus alone deserves worship, not Caesar.

Festus listens and sees the point, but concludes that Paul is mad (v. 24). Agrippa hesitates, although he seems to feel the attraction of the gospel (v. 28). They picture differing, negative responses. Amid these reactions, Paul's responsibility is simply to speak the gospel faithfully and leave the rest in God's hands.

4 Faith and fear at sea

Acts 27:1–32

Paul's journey to Rome is covered by Jesus' promise that Paul will testify there (23:11)—but the sea journey is far from straightforward. Even today, we know the power of sea storms and are cautious about sea travel when storms threaten. The ancients viewed the sea as dangerous, and storms with terror. Their wooden boats were vulnerable and many lives were lost in the trading ships that crisscrossed the Mediterranean. Luke travels with Paul here (notice 'we' in verse 1) and tells a vivid story.

'The Fast' (v. 9) is the Jewish Day of Atonement, which falls in late September/early October, so presumably Paul observed it in Fair Havens, on Crete. The danger period for sea travel was 14 September to 11 November; after that, no one travelled by sea until the spring. Paul recognises this seasonal danger and seeks to persuade the centurion who is accompanying him to wait, but the centurion is not to be delayed (vv. 10–11). They leave Fair Havens (vv. 7–8) and make for Phoenix, further round the Cretan coast (v. 12), but the journey is never to be completed. A powerful wind causes a storm and sweeps the ship along for days (vv. 13–20).

How does Paul respond in faith to these frightening events? After saying, 'I told you so' (v. 21), he calls them to faith in the God he serves: even in a storm, Paul's instincts are to share his faith and invite others to join him as believers. Paul tells them of the angel's promise (vv. 23–24) and of his confidence in God (v. 25), and warns them that it still won't be 'plain sailing' (v. 26). God isn't promising them an easy journey, but he is promising them a safe arrival.

Even so, fear overcomes some of the sailors—perhaps understandably, for they were probably far more experienced seafarers than Paul. They try to escape in a small rowing boat (v. 30), and it takes a sharp warning from Paul, that the whole crew needs to stay together to be saved, to prevent them from leaving (vv. 31–32). Paul stands with these people, in some ways exercising faith on their behalf, in the confidence that God will be true to his promises. Here is a model worth reflecting on.

5 More threats—and more protection

Acts 27:33—28:10

Paul continues to face threats to his safety, but his confidence in God is great amid this danger. After two weeks adrift, just as he did earlier in the storm, he encourages his shipmates and assures them that the journey will be safe—and he gives thanks to God as he himself eats (27:33–36). This food will sustain them through the final stages of the doomed voyage as the ship runs aground and breaks up (v. 41).

Here is yet another threat to Paul—from the soldiers, who fear the prisoners will escape. The soldiers know that they will face the punishment that the prisoners were due if they do escape (v. 42), so killing the prisoners is an option, since the soldiers will then be safe. God protects Paul again, this time through the centurion who guards him, Julius (27:1). Julius prevents the soldiers from acting violently and saves Paul: perhaps he has responded in faith to the gospel, or perhaps he is simply a man concerned for justice.

The island where they fetch up is Malta (28:1), where danger appears again, in the form of a snake. Although there are no poisonous snakes on Malta today, there may have been in Roman times. (Compare the situation in Ireland, where snakes are said to have been driven out by St Patrick: this shows that people remembered the presence of snakes there.) God once again protects Paul from danger: his promise is dependable (23:11).

Malta is under Roman control, governed by the 'First Man', Publius (28:7: NRSV's 'leading man' misses the fact that this is a title, attested in inscriptions). God opens a door for the gospel when Paul successfully prays for healing for Publius' father, who is seriously ill, and other healings follow (v. 9). It is striking that Paul prays for this man with no mention of prior gospel preaching. Indeed, Luke does not say whether Publius or his father ever came to faith: healing is God's gracious and gratuitous gift to them.

Maltese tradition dates the planting of its church to this visit by Paul, and that seems probable. Among the difficulties of this horrendous sea journey, God is at work drawing people to himself through Paul and his companions.

6 Finally, Rome!

Acts 28:11–31

Acts closes in Rome, the capital and heart of the empire. Paul is given the relative freedom of house arrest, able to receive visitors (vv. 16, 30), perhaps because Festus' advice was that the charges against him were unlikely to be upheld (25:25–27).

We might expect Paul to be preparing for his trial in Rome—but none of it! His primary concern is still his mission from Jesus, so he calls the Jewish leaders of Rome to meet him (v. 17). He explains his presence there and seeks to counter any accusations that they might have heard brought against him (vv. 17–20). Being under arrest was itself dishonourable—'innocent until proven guilty' was not a Roman belief—so Paul would be assumed to be a criminal. Furthermore, for anyone to spend time with Paul could make them dishonourable by association. The Jews had been expelled from Rome not many years earlier (18:2), so, although they were back in the city, they needed to be careful about their reputation.

These Jewish leaders are open people: they have not heard bad things about Paul, but they have heard accusations against the Christian 'sect' (v. 22), so they want to hear from Paul about the gospel. Paul needs no second invitation! He spends a whole day with them, speaking from the scriptures about Jesus and the kingdom of God (v. 23). Luke 'bookends' the whole of Acts here, for Acts began with Jesus himself speaking of the kingdom of God (1:3). As in other places, the gospel divides the Jewish community: some accept it, but others do not (v. 24).

Some commentators see Paul's quotation from Isaiah 6:9–10 (vv. 26–27), in combination with verse 28, finally shutting the door on the possibility of Jews coming to faith in Jesus. This is unlikely, for Paul's equally definite-sounding 'We turn to the Gentiles' statements in 13:46 and 18:6 are followed by reports of his entering the synagogue in another city (14:1; 19:8). The Isaiah quotation is indeed a solemn warning, echoing the brief quotation from Isaiah 6:9 in the parable of the soils (Luke 8:4–15; the quotation is in verse 10). The Roman Jews are warned, as are Luke's readers, of the need to hear and respond to the gospel of Jesus, spoken by his witnesses in the power of the Spirit (v. 25).

Guidelines

Luke portrays the captive, confined Paul in the final quarter of Acts. This portrait invites reflection on how we deal with limitations.

Paul faces limitations imposed from outside: he is under arrest and under Roman guard for much of Acts 21—28. Some believers today face such pressure daily, especially where their faith is unwelcome or rejected. In 2014 this was true particularly in parts of Syria and Iraq, where the so-called Islamic State forces attacked and killed Christians. Paul's portrait here calls us to pray for such people, that just as the Lord upheld and guarded Paul, he would do the same for believers who face similar external pressures and limitations. Paul's portrait also calls us to pray that our fellow believers under pressure will be faithful to Christ and bear testimony to him amid their limitations, as Paul did in prison and on trial. To learn more about the suffering church and gain fuel for prayer, visit the website of Christian Solidarity Worldwide (www.csw.org.uk).

Limitations come from within, too: we sometimes impose our own limitations because of fear. Western culture today is gradually marginalising the life of faith, and this can cause Christian people to feel threatened and to step back from living and speaking their faith. We may fail to be open about our faith because we fear others' response. It's worth reflecting on and praying about how our faith touches our 'frontline', the place where we spend the majority of our life—our work, our home, our school, college or university, or somewhere else. How inhibited do we feel, and how much do we hold back from being openly Christian in such situations? Pray for God's grace and the Spirit's power to engage Christianly with your frontline day by day.

A third group of limitations are those of age and disability. When your body or mind won't do what it used to do and what you still want it to do, it is frustrating and can lead to despair. Paul's example, with the limitations of his imprisonment, invites us to consider how God can use us, and how we can honour Jesus, in our response to these limitations. Godliness can and will shine through as we respond to God in this way—and others' lives will be touched.

FURTHER READING

Beverly R. Gaventa, *Acts* (NT Commentary series), Abingdon Press, 2003.
Tom Wright, *Acts for Everyone* (two volumes), SPCK, 2008.

Malachi

The title tells us nothing about the prophet's identity. 'Malachi' is a straight transliteration of the Hebrew for 'my messenger'. The content of the book tells us little more. The date, however, c.500–450BC (on which scholars are agreed), tells us a lot. After 50 years of indifferent kingship, the arrival of the boy-king Josiah in 637BC brought a wind of change to a dispirited people, fortified in 621BC by Hilkaiah's discovery of 'the Book of the Law' (substantially Deuteronomy), a discovery that set off a programme of religious, social and cultural reform. Sadly, before the reforms had a chance to become established in the community, other events intervened.

In 586 the Babylonians invaded, sacked Jerusalem, destroyed the temple and carried off the cream of the population to Babylon, where most of them remained until the Persians overcame the Babylonians and enabled their return to the homeland. However, the years of return were not straightforward.

When Malachi arrived on the scene, everything was at rock bottom. The community was divided and dispirited, and natural disasters and a stalled economy had led to universal scepticism. What Malachi offers is a difficult Hebrew text, not immediately relevant to today's world. Appreciating it therefore calls for a degree of supposition and creative imagination—not the sort of imagination that fantasises about things that never existed but the sort that enables a fresh look at a familiar situation.

One way is to begin with the writer rather than the text. To speak (or write) as he does suggests a strong religious experience; from the little we know (an unidentified person, in a tough spot, with a dispirited people, trying to hear the voice of God), we will try to unpack that experience. Imagine the text as the fruit of his daily prayers, wrestling with the problems of the day and bringing different issues to the fore.

Because our world is different from Malachi's, there is little point in trying to draw parallels. However, as we say our prayers, his experience may ring bells, and the word we hear may not be a word from Malachi but a word from the Lord. We are to read him, therefore, with our feet on the ground as we walk in his shoes, always with one eye on what is happening around us, learning to see and yearning to hear.

Quotations are taken from the New Revised Standard Version.

1 The vastness of God

Malachi 1:2–5

Malachi's question is: where is God and what is he doing? Does he still love us? (Evidence is thin on the ground.) If he does, why doesn't he show us?

Malachi is surrounded by people who continue the traditional religious rituals and believe in one God. Some of them assume that God's dominion ranges far beyond the borders of Israel, but, after hundreds of years, they still can't get on with their closest relatives and long-standing neighbours, the Edomites. Strife between near neighbours is not unknown and usually has a history. Relations with Edom soured way back in the days of Jacob and Esau, so they had never been good, and in Malachi's day they were at a particularly low ebb. By this time, Jerusalem was going through the mill and Edom was on a bit of an up. A mixture of past rivalry and jealousy, plus limited and unequal resources, served only to accentuate the problem.

How can Malachi or anyone else believe in a God of love when, at the same time, they take it for granted that God hates a particular part of his creation as much as they do? Whether Yahweh really did hate Edom is questionable, but there is no doubt that the Jews did.

From where we sit, it may all seem a bit remote—a storm in a teacup, perhaps—but not for a Jew or an Edomite in the sixth century BC. Edom burns with resentment; Judah, as always, maintains her superiority. Both sides have a point. Solutions, plans and compromises should not be too difficult to find and there is no shortage of volunteer problem-solvers, but Malachi is not a social worker or a counsellor with a mission to hear the arguments.

Malachi has a different fire in his belly. Starting from a different place, he burns with fire on behalf of a God whose vision is much vaster. Malachi's remit is way beyond that of dealing with two squabbling parties, be they brothers, sisters, neighbouring churches, faiths or nations.

Religious experience begins with that kind of God and a commitment to him.

2 As God sees it

Malachi 1:6–10

There is a chasm between Malachi's vision of God and the pettiness of the people, whose God is too small. If this was the trigger that got him going, the next stage is the chasm between Malachi and those who reject (or ignore) God—not just the people in general but also those whose calling it is to protect and proclaim God. Malachi is a square peg surrounded by round holes, unable to reconcile his approach with that of his contemporaries and religious leaders. So where is he coming from?

Malachi grew up under the shadow of the book of Deuteronomy, especially chapters 12—26, often thought to be the foundation of the reform programme that followed Hilkaiah's discovery of the Book of the Law in the temple. This book emphasised humanity, individual responsibility, motive and intention, equality and justice, especially towards the weaker members of society—a million miles away from the experience of those weaker members. The reforms may never have caught on, leaving a nation split between those who continued to hope and those who either had never known or had forgotten what their society was meant to be.

How did the situation appear to a sensitive soul who tried to see it as it must have looked to God? Basic respect for God hardly seems to have been top of the agenda for the religious leaders. In a tough economy, everybody fights for their own advantage. Priests cut corners and, with their survival at stake, indulged in practices which anyone in the Malachi tradition would have found objectionable. The current priesthood, hardly the flavour of the month anyway, must have been something of a *bête noire* to a character like Malachi, committed to reform.

Relations between priests and Levites during this period are perhaps best explained in terms of the difference between those who majored on rituals, institutions and sacrifice and those who were more committed to the word and social justice. Malachi is firmly on the side of the word and social justice, reflecting Deuteronomy and much of the prophetic tradition that sprang from it. Something in Malachi tells him it is time for a wake-up call.

What of our own situations? Avoid the historical details of Malachi's world; focus rather on your world as God sees it and start from there.

3 A fresh start

Malachi 1:11–14

In his daily prayer, Malachi opens his eyes and sees what he has never noticed before. How come other people, in other nations and with other gods, seem not to have the same problem as Israel (v. 11)? 'Nations' suggests those outside Judaism, whose names for God and responses to God are totally different, but who still respect his will and maintain their faith. Meanwhile, people 'within' Judaism are so busy pursuing their own interests that they seem to neither know nor care; even among the best of them, there is a deep gulf between what they profess (if they profess anything at all) and their general lifestyle.

Whether Malachi's impression is fair is questionable. It may be partly exaggeration, fantasy, star-gazing or the fruit of a bad day at the office, but his impression may still ring bells for us. If so, we do ourselves a disservice if we dismiss it without further reflection. Even allowing for a touch of hyperbole, might it not be significant that, whereas Malachi finds himself in a dying and decaying world, he is well aware that religion is flourishing in other countries? Might it be that, at home, the focus is on the wrong issues or expressed in the wrong way? Or is it that those with the audacity to focus everything on a particular understanding of God in relation to their traditions are failing to recognise many much more fundamental issues calling for the attention of God's people?

To Malachi, God's ire seems to be reserved for the professionals, but today perhaps we should think more of pressures (or, we might say, 'education') from families, friends, the media, business and commerce. Equality, fairness and justice in the book of Deuteronomy and replicated in more personal terms in the teaching of Jesus, especially in Luke, are universal and challenge us all. What matters is not what we say (vv. 12, 14) but what we do, and not only what we say with words but also what we say with our attitudes. Body language is not a new invention. As from the lips of God, Malachi's word is one of woe to a society whose lifestyle is totally out of kilter with what it professes.

4 The covenant of Levi

Daily prayers may be thought of as a safeguard against the unwelcome intrusions of the devil, but this is not so. Malachi hears a call to give up on the current outfit—the priests. The system no longer works; the contemporary occupants have lost the plot.

Whatever might have made this deeply committed man entertain such heretical ideas? Perhaps he came at the end of a long line of prophets and others who felt the same way. For 500 years (as long as between the Reformation and today) his people had been wrestling with the idea of God, and what comes across to us as a relatively seamless history was nothing like that for anyone who knew even a little of the story.

Those 500 years were years of turmoil, with varying emphases and traditions rising and falling, some brief, some long-standing, as every generation pursued its own interests. Once in a while, a fresh idea or a person (a prophet or a ruler) would come along and hold the stage, leaving a mark on history but changing little. Rulers changed; empires came and went. Praying against that background, for Malachi, who was always closer to the laity than to the professionals, one question was likely to dominate: whatever happened to the covenant of Levi (v. 4)?

Since this covenant features nowhere else, we don't know much about it, but history suggests tensions between the Levites (possibly subordinate temple officials, akin to the prophets with a commitment to the word) and the priests (whose primary occupation was the altar and sacrifice). Think of distinctions today between priest and minister, or clergy and laity, and add in Deuteronomy's Levi—something of a 'father-figure', an icon of correctness, faithfulness and reliability.

What, then, might Malachi have had in mind? Fundamentally, reverence for God, for the world he created and the values required to keep it alive, alongside respect for the people and the need for teaching and instruction on all those values. The people may not want it, and certainly not from the priests, but what they don't need is false teaching or teaching from an aristocracy who show little regard in their personal lives for what they teach.

5 The covenant of our ancestors (1)

Malachi 2:10–15

Superficially this text seems easier, but is it? Scholars have unpacked some of the finer points but, since it is uncertain precisely what Malachi said (or wrote) and even less clear what he meant by it, it would be wrong to draw questionable ethical conclusions and relate them to our own day. It is better to start with a different question—not 'What did Malachi actually say and mean?' but 'What particular religious experience might have prompted this message as a word from the Lord?'

What might Malachi have meant by 'profaning the covenant of our ancestors' (v. 10)? The very phrase calls us to be sensitive to those who have gone before and faithful to what we have inherited. To what extent do we keep alive the things for which they fought and, in some cases, died? Do we think hard before changing or discarding them? Worse than forgetting, to what extent do we keep the 'memories' alive with occasional or regular rituals and ceremonies, while ignoring or deliberately flouting them the rest of the time?

Malachi's world, remember, was very mixed. There were two, if not three, minority communities struggling for survival in the context of an oppressive culture—Jews returning from Babylon, Jews who had never been to Babylon, and Babylonians (presumably a minority) who saw migration as an opportunity to 'move house' or 'improve their quality of life'. Hence the tension between those who had stayed behind and adjusted, bearing the hardships and weathering the storms, and those who had returned and were looking for 'the old world' (which was no longer there). The latter might be critical of those who had never left, or anxious to bring their Babylonian experience to bear in order to build an entirely new community round a new temple. They brought new ideas, not altogether popular.

At this point, Malachi seems to have little positive to say, but that may be his message. He probably has friends and contacts in all camps, is unsure where he is or what he can do about it, and is unclear about what Yahweh would like him to do. It's easy to appreciate his dilemma, but, without going through the hoops in thought and prayer, he is unlikely ever to find out what he should do next.

6 The covenant of our ancestors (2)

Malachi 2:11–16

In Malachi's time, family life was under threat. Some, following the tradition of Solomon, had married foreign wives. Deliberately or accidentally, with foreign wives came foreign faiths and, in due course, 'mixed infants'—not sure where they belonged and a prey to those who wanted to 'claim' them. If taking a foreign wife meant first abandoning the wife they already had, there were further consequences, not least for the women involved. These verses suggest a man wrestling with the issues in the light of his past and present situations and how it all looked to God.

Some scholars have suggested that these verses may be read as a word for the community rather than the individual, which is an aspect worth exploring. Malachi would have been familiar with the idea that Yahweh could be regarded as a bridegroom, with Israel as his bride (see, for example, Isaiah 62:5)—not unlike the gods of the surrounding nations, who often had consorts. Faithlessness on the part of the people, then, would put Yahweh in the role of a deserted husband, so it would come as no surprise to be reminded that Yahweh hates divorce (v. 16).

But might Malachi be on to something more profound? The Hebrew word translated as 'divorce' is capable of a wider interpretation than simply a split between husband and wife. Yahweh's people have given up one way of life (their first love) for another, and Yahweh doesn't like it. A different but equally acceptable translation for 'God hates divorce', therefore, may be 'God hates separation'—that is, a break between two things that belong together. Separated, neither can produce true offspring.

This puts faithfulness and respect for the past, and the matter of separation, in a different context, with the focus less on personal family life and more on the whole community. This community appears to have lost its roots, and has broken not only the relationship but the heart of God into the bargain. Malachi feels for what has been lost and either mourns or is angered by the treatment of the God he loves.

There is no solution to the problem, or resolution to the conflict, but at least the foundations are being thoughtfully and prayerfully laid for what is to come.

Guidelines

- 'One reason for reading the Bible is its ability to have something to say on the topics of our day. When we bring *our* questions to the Bible we often see in clearer focus what might have been only a dim reflection had we started from the other end, trying to understand the Bible in some abstract theoretical way and then trying to apply it to life today. In this way we engage in a two-way process, leading to new angles on how scripture can still speak to us on matters that its original authors could never have imagined' (John Drane, *Bible in Transmission*, Bible Society, Summer 2014, p. 11). Keep this in your mind every day as we go through Malachi.
- How big is your God, and how does he compare with the God of your friends, your particular tradition or your neighbours?
- Do you sense a chasm between your view of the world and the world-view of employers, politicians, the media, creative artists or many of your acquaintances? If you do, can you clarify why it is and what, if anything, you can do about it?
- Can you identify anything which God might 'hate' today because two things that belong together and depend on each other have been separated? When? By whom? And with what consequences?
- What happened to the dreams and hopes for a better world that inspired you five, ten or 20 years ago?

16–22 November

1 A word for the children of Levi

Malachi 2:17—3:5

Perhaps Malachi has had a bad night, but, as often after a bad night, his waking moments are moments of clarity. Or perhaps, after saying his morning prayers, he opens his eyes, takes one more look outside, and sighs. In spite of all that he and others have said and done, the masses seem no longer able to get it. This time the object of his disappointment is 'the children of Levi' (v. 3), who claim to delight in the 'covenant'. In other words, the reformers seem as lost as everybody else. They still ask,

'What have we done wrong? How did we ever get here?' Surely somebody somewhere should be putting things right. Malachi tells them plainly: they have misread the situation, asked the wrong questions, and lost touch with a God of justice (2:17).

To begin with, Malachi can only pin his hopes on a conviction that, one day, all those causing the problem and all who fail to act for what they know to be right—including the so-called reformers—will get their comeuppance, and it will not be a pleasant sight. Pause to think what he had in mind with 'a refiner's fire' and 'fullers' soap'.

Who is he talking about? Malachi is very specific (3:5). He names four groups in particular:

- The 'sorcerers', who may be false prophets, crying peace when there is no peace, or seeing the world through rose-coloured spectacles and noticing only what is good for them.
- The 'adulterers', who exploit what is good or beautiful and either poison it or destroy it altogether.
- The 'oppressors', who pay low wages to hired (contract?) workers.
- The 'widows, orphans and aliens'—a whole range of people who have nobody to support or protect them, who don't fit the system (that is, conform to the norm) and are never to the fore when the prizes are being handed out.

Does it ring any bells?

In one verse, then, we have a summary of the book of Deuteronomy and the Magnificat, presenting an agenda big enough to busy the church of today for years to come.

2 A touch of remorse

Malachi 3:6–12

The shock of yesterday's reading may not have gone away, but the emphasis now changes. Previously Malachi focused on the people responsible; here, perhaps after time to reflect, he is more positive. If only people could see that, despite all the errors of their ways, God is always much more faithful to them than they are to him! If Malachi can get that across to them, maybe (just maybe) it will inspire a touch of remorse. It's worth a try, but they need help with the 'how', and the starting point is to face up to where they have gone wrong. Malachi drops a few hints.

- First, their total disregard for history. It's not so much their failure to learn from experience (though that is part of it) as their total loss of the fundamentals—Moses and the covenant of Sinai, through Elijah and Ahab, on to the eighth-century prophets (Amos and Micah in particular), and coming to a head with those Deuteronomic reforms whose high hopes and moral tone were either ignored, neglected or thwarted.
- Second, their failure to appreciate that 'the Lord does not change' or (to put it differently) that fundamentals such as love, care, understanding and forgiveness are universal human values, unchangeable because they are rooted in the heart of God, in whose image we are all made. To reject them is to reject God.
- Third, their defaulting in tithes and offering. This is more than just neglecting church maintenance. According to Deuteronomy 14:28–29, tithes could be used for social purposes, and, if people of substance paid them, they could provide adequate provision for the socially oppressed (Malachi 3:5). That of itself would be a practical commitment to becoming the children of one father and creator (2:10). If the people have lost touch with the God of justice and fairness (2:17), it is only because they have given up on him, not vice versa.
- Fourth, their apparent failure to understand that what Yahweh can do depends on what we do. 'You play your part, I will play mine,' Yahweh seems to say. His creation is more than capable of providing for all, adapting and renewing itself when it fails, but it is not helped if we continually interfere and exploit it for our own benefit.

3 Morning sunshine

Malachi 3:13–18

For Malachi, this is the sort of morning when the sun shines but is quickly followed by light cloud. After days of gloom, the sun comes out: people start to ask questions. Previously it was only the priests who were asking (1:6), because they were the principal objects of God's (or Malachi's) wrath, and their questions were religious questions. Now the people too realise that they need guidance on where they are failing, but their questions are different—and this is where the weather gets murky again. First comes a question based on self-satisfaction: what are they going to get out of serving God (v. 14)? But others follow: how come arrogance pays and evildoers get away with it (v. 15)? These are not, I would suggest, the questions that Malachi wants to address, at least not directly—maybe because he is becoming aware of a change in the atmosphere and doesn't want to lose his audience.

How much time elapsed between verses 15 and 16 can only be a matter of speculation, but now the sun returns, and with increasing brightness. There is no evidence that anything has changed but Malachi is a different man. Perhaps the sun was always there, perhaps not, but now he sees it as never before. People have started talking to one another, and, once people meet and talk, miracles can happen. This is the key to the difference between 'the righteous' and 'the wicked'. Sadly for us, before we discover what they talk about, what changes are made and how, the light goes out, the curtain comes down and we are compelled to speculate or to look in a mirror.

Like any good drama, chapter 3 leaves us with more questions than solutions, but we, the readers, have to write the next act for ourselves. Taken to the brook and offered the running water, it is we who have to drink.

Who were (or are) the people who 'revered the Lord' (v. 16)? What did they talk about? What did they hear? Again, we can only speculate, but the conclusions they reached are less important than our answers to the same issues. Even more important is the change of heart and approach, which challenges us. This is *our* second chance, the key to discovering the truth that Malachi and Yahweh care about.

4 Down from the mount

Malachi 4:1–5

After yesterday's climax, there has to be a comedown. Maybe next day, maybe next month or even years later, it is still the case that little has changed. Even small communities, like Judah, change but slowly, as the subsequent work of Ezra and Nehemiah testifies, and verses 1–3 have a touch of unreality about them. 'If only...' is not an inappropriate response.

However, the scene is not the same—or, if it is, Malachi and probably many others are seeing it differently. Try reading these verses and concepts as poetry. Facts, figures and reality come second to dreams and emotions. We are back with the Israelites, albeit still in the wilderness but with a vision of a land always drawing them on (Isaiah 55:12–13), like any nation emerging from years of turmoil and subject to a foreign power.

In John Steinbeck's *The Red Pony*, Grandfather tells the story of 'westering'—how he led the people through the desert lands to the west coast. Westering, he says, was 'one big crawling beast... every man wanted something for himself, but the big beast that was all of them wanted only westering'. When they saw the mountains, they cried, but it wasn't getting there that mattered; it was movement—'westering'. When they got to the sea, there was nowhere else to go and 'westering' died. It wasn't a hunger any more.

At the heart of Malachi is the dream and the hunger, although not every brick will be in place at the same time and much of it will only ever emerge in God's time.

Is this, then, the key to the change in Malachi? Not necessarily the realisation of the hopes they started with but a fresh understanding of what set it all off—Moses, Elijah and the prophets. The Hebrew Bible comes to an end with the Law and the Prophets, but not without paving the way in the Christian Bible for the emergence of a new Elijah in the figure of John the Baptist, and much else.

5 What manner of man?

Luke 1:46–55

One way of appreciating a prophet is to look at what happened next. That brings us to the Gospels, in particular to Luke and the Magnificat. Another 500 years have come and gone but the spirit that inspired Malachi is still around and bearing fruit.

Try putting together a picture of Malachi the man, with nothing to go on but his writings. You might imagine a fairly ordinary, traditional and unprepossessing Jewish man, with a deep concern for his contemporaries and for the faith he has inherited. He has no great skills or flights of oratory but has more than an average dose of nous or common sense. With a broad understanding of history and tradition, his heart warms to (even burns for) the days and the hopes of Deuteronomic reform. If the health of a community is to be judged by the way it treats the underdog, then Malachi is your man, with a respect for leadership, even though he is deeply disappointed in the current incumbents and is not afraid to say so.

Try once again to walk in his shoes. Identify one or two points where you sensed a kindred spirit and consider how his experience can rouse and stimulate you. Now reverse the roles and imagine Malachi in your shoes. How differently might his message come out? If he were in your shoes, how might he respond? What would he say?

Is this where Luke found himself when confronted with Mary, as he tried to walk in her shoes? Commentators have not been slow to see the Magnificat as reflecting Hannah's song (1 Samuel 2:1–10), though there is no evidence that Hannah or Mary ever saw these words as anything more than their own personal stories. To this Luke adds the sentiments of Deuteronomy (individual responsibility, equality and justice)—so deep a concern of Malachi—thereby giving us the fruit of Luke's own religious experience, which has been such an inspiration in so many different ways to countless readers ever since.

If you cannot find the key to a renewed hope in the *word* of the prophet, try spotting the *experience* of the prophet in which he hears 'the word of the Lord', and open your heart to a similar experience.

6 What manner of community?

Luke 1:67–79

After attempting a picture of Malachi, try now to draw a picture of the community, sticking mainly to Malachi's topics. Avoid the temptation to see Malachi as the end of an era and John the Baptist (or his father, Zechariah) as the beginning of a new. Try to see both as delicately placed on the cusp of history.

Both are facing a divided community. Malachi has to deal with those who are returning from exile in Babylon, disappointed reformers with probably unrealistic expectations, while Zechariah's society faces Roman domination, Judaism in turmoil, internal dissent (Sadducees versus Pharisees) and reforming Essene communities who are waiting in the wings.

Both live in fear of their enemies and suffer limitations on the life they want to lead (vv. 71–73, 75). Both have a past that they want to maintain, and both respect the challenge of the new (v. 72). Leadership is divided, not altogether committed to what the community is looking for, and words like 'mercy' and 'forgiveness' trip easily off the tongue but lack substance in reality. Peace is the goal, seeking light in the darkness (v. 79).

Most of us live in communities that are similar in many ways to those of Malachi and Zechariah. The more we look at their world, the more we realise that, confused though the picture may be, we have a choice. We can at least open our eyes to see as they saw, even if the details are different; to hear as they heard, even if the words are different; and to make our own response in the light of 'what happened next'—what they did, or failed to do, and with what consequences.

Making our choice will remind us that 'religious experience' is something much more than a warm feeling of satisfaction. True religious experience holds the key to change and a better world, whether it be through the wider sweep of history (Wilberforce on slavery, Carey on the mission field or Martin Luther King with a dream) or simply in our own personal families, offices, shops or streets. And sometimes the consequences can be more far-reaching than we realise at the time, as when Rosa Parks, in 1955, refused to give up her seat on the bus to a white man, thus putting down a significant marker in the USA's Civil Rights Movement.

Guidelines

- Identify 'the children of Levi' around you, and reflect on your feelings about them in relation to your understanding of a God of justice.
- Can you distinguish between the loss of a past that we simply miss and the loss of those things which have had far-reaching, often unintended, consequences? Is there anything we can do to restore or replace those lost things?
- Meditate on your dreams. Where do they come from and how can you keep them alive? How can we maintain the thrill of the dream and the

journey, without looking for a perfect solution to every obstacle that gets in the way? Remember that sometimes it is enough simply to cherish them and be thankful.

- We began by suggesting that one key to Malachi was to 'walk in his shoes'—but there is a further step to take. When Scout is having difficulty with her teacher and classmates in Harper Lee's *To Kill a Mocking Bird*, her father says, 'You never really understand a person until you consider things from his point of view—until you climb into his skin and walk around in it.' That is even more demanding.

FURTHER READING

R.J. Coggins, *Haggai, Zechariah, Malachi* (Old Testament Guides), Sheffield Academic Press, 1987.

Paul L. Redditt, *Haggai, Zechariah, Malachi* (New Century Bible Commentary), Marshall Pickering, 1995.

J.W. Rogerson and Judith M. Lieu (eds), *The Oxford Handbook of Biblical Studies*, Oxford University Press, 2006.

Charles M Laymon (ed.), *The Interpreter's One Volume Bible Commentary*, Abingdon Press, 1971.

Jo Blenkinsopp, *A History of Prophecy in Israel*, Westminster Press, 1996.

Bruce C. Birch, *Let Justice Roll Down*, Westminster/John Knox Press, 1991.

Romans

Romans is justly celebrated as one of the most profound and influential New Testament documents. We approach it with an excitement about exposure to Paul's mature articulation of the good news of what God has done in Christ and an awareness that its profundity does not exclude some complexities that continue to provoke debate among interpreters. The next three weeks will allow us to read through the whole letter. The brief comments on extended passages will focus on attempting to clarify the flow of its argument and will, of course, only touch the surface. For more thorough treatments or alternative viewpoints, any of the books listed at the end under 'Further reading' are worth consulting.

Paul wrote his great exposition of the gospel in the late 50s of the first century, from Corinth, to Christians in Rome. It is by no means a theological treatise in the abstract but is shaped by his reflections on both his own and his readers' situation. It is, therefore, both a missional and a pastoral document, arising from and supporting his mission to the Gentiles and geared to persuading Roman Christians to provide unified backing of his further mission to Spain (see 15:28–29). To gain that backing among believers in a place where he had not himself visited or founded a church (1:9–13), he sets out his message in a way designed to enable them to overcome objections to it that they may share, as well as the problems that have arisen because of differences between their Jewish and Gentile members (14:1—15:13).

The rehearsal of Paul's gospel that emerges from this setting is breathtaking in its scope. Its vision of God's universal purposes embraces God's justice and love, how these are demonstrated in the death and resurrection of Jesus, the plight of humanity that must have required this solution, the inauguration of a new humanity, the consummation of the whole creation, God's faithfulness to Israel in this process, and the formation of communities of love and justice that participate in God's continuing mission in the world. It is little wonder, then, that Romans still captures the imagination and has transformative effects as readers engage with the impact and implications of its message.

Unless otherwise indicated, quotations are taken from the New Revised Standard Version of the Bible.

1 God's gospel and Paul's mission

Romans 1:1–17

What connects Paul with the letter's recipients and justifies his writing to them? The link is God's good news. Paul's identity and vocation are determined by the good about God's Son, from whom he has received a distinctive commission. This gospel fulfils the promises of the Jewish scriptures and concerns Jesus as the Messiah. At the same time, Jesus' resurrection through the Spirit now brings the nations under his Lordship. The Gentiles are the focus of Paul's apostolic assignment, and so the predominantly Gentile Christians in Rome are included within its scope.

Paul sees the goal of gospel proclamation as an authentic faith characterised by obedience to Christ (v. 5) within firmly established churches. He is eager, therefore, to proclaim the gospel to his readers (v. 15) and immediately proceeds to do just that, beginning with the thematic statement of verses 16–17.

Paul is confident that the gospel is more than just another set of teachings about life. Instead, as the vehicle of the same force that raised Jesus from the dead, establishing his Sonship (v. 4), it constitutes the divine power at work to rescue and transform the world. This becomes effective when appropriated through faith, a means that is available to all, both Jews and Gentiles.

In the gospel, the righteousness or justice of God is disclosed. In the Jewish scriptures, as here, God's salvation and just judgment are often paralleled, highlighting how God, in faithfulness to the covenant, puts the world to rights, rescuing God's people and restoring well-being. Again, such action is appropriated by faith, so Paul interprets Habakkuk 2:4 to assert that the one who, through faith, has experienced God's just judgment will have life (v. 17). This thought will shape the rest of the letter. Romans 1:18—4:25 deals with the revelation of God's righteousness and justification by faith, and 9:1—11:36 with whether these are indeed in line with God's faithfulness to Israel, while 5:1 —8:39 and 12:1-—15:13 explore individual and communal participation in the inaugurated life of the age to come. The backdrop for this terminology is the contrast in Jewish thought between life in this age and in the age to come, accomplished by God's end-time judgement. In the age to come, there would be peace instead of violence, wholeness instead of disease, abundance instead of dearth, and life in place of death. Paul sees this life as having already begun through the divine judgement expressed in Christ's death and resurrection.

2 God's wrath and humanity's inexcusable folly

Romans 1:18–32

Having introduced the gospel's revelation of God's justice and the life that proceeds from it, Paul talks now, in what may seem an abrupt shift, of the revelation of God's wrath, which will be a recurring topic (2:5, 8; 3:5; 5:9; 9:22; 12:19; 13:4–5). But, since he has stated that salvation is for all, both Jew and Gentile, he needs to show why it is that all are in need of this solution to their plight. Without it, both groups within humanity, because of their alienation from God and resulting evils, deserve God's wrath. That wrath is not some arbitrary or tyrannical vengeance but simply the reverse side of the salvific justice that is the content of the good news. Faced with all forms of sin and injustice, God's righteous judgment is revealed in fierce condemnation.

Most of Paul's indictment of human wickedness is an adaptation of the language and thought of Wisdom of Solomon 12—14, where it reflects a Hellenistic Jewish perspective on God's just verdict on Gentile idolatry and immorality and God's mercy towards Israel. Paul, however, will employ it in a 'sting operation' to show that those who hold this typical view of Gentiles fall victim to their own indictment of others (see 2:1).

Wisdom of Solomon asserts that, in their attitude to God, the nations are foolish and without excuse (Wisdom 13:1–9). Paul reinforces this analysis. The transcendent God is present and active within creation, and that creation, including humans, displays this reality. Humans have known this truth but have twisted and suppressed it in an attempt to escape it. It is not that neutral reasoning has failed to find God but that failure to acknowledge God has led to futile thinking, 'so they are without excuse' (v. 20). Its folly is that, instead of orienting their existence around the Creator, humans end up making some finite aspect of creation ultimate, thereby becoming enslaved to it (vv. 23, 25).

Idolatry leads to immorality and evil, and three times Paul indicates that God gave humans up to this process (vv. 24, 26, 28). It is not simply that sin has its own consequences but, rather, that God's activity is to be discerned in those consequences. The revelation of God's wrath consists in giving humans what they choose, with all its entailments.

3 God's impartial wrath and Jewish culpability

Romans 2

By including sins such as envy, deceit, gossip, boastfulness and heartless-ness, Paul's earlier list of Gentile vices (1:29–31) extended beyond idola-try and what Wisdom of Solomon and other ancient moralists considered unnatural sexual acts because they involved excessive lust. Paul therefore has no difficulty in turning the tables and showing that those who make moral judgements about others are condemning themselves. By verse 17 it becomes clear that the person who judges, the imaginary interlocutor to whom these comments are initially addressed (vv. 1, 3), has reference primarily to a Jewish representative.

Paul challenges the presumption of the attitude expressed in Wisdom of Solomon 12—14, where God's wrath falls on the Gentiles but Israel simply experiences God's fatherly chastisement and mercy. He does so by underscoring two basic divine characteristics. The first is God's kindness, of which Wisdom of Solomon itself says, 'You overlook people's sins, so that they may repent' (11:23). The second is asserted, for example, in Deuteronomy 10:17: 'The Lord your God… is not partial.' Unrepented Jewish sins and God's impartial judgement of the deeds of both Jews and Gentiles lead to God's wrath for those who imagine themselves exempt (Romans 2:5, 8).

In describing God's judgement on the basis of whether people do good or evil (vv. 9–13), Paul has in view the principle, and not whether anyone actually succeeds in gaining eternal life through good deeds. Once that question is raised, however, his answer will be overwhelmingly clear: there is no one who does good and is vindicated by God on this basis

(3:10, 20). But at this point, Paul's talk of God's impartial judgement according to deeds is designed to drive home the message that neither having the Torah nor possessing the identity marker of circumcision will suffice as a protection against God's wrath. What counts before God is the actual performance of the requirements of the law, which comes from the heart.

Paul leaves no doubt that the final righteous judgement forms part of the good news: 'according to my gospel... through Jesus Christ' (v. 16). To anyone who suspects that his talk of justification by faith shortchanges God's justice, Paul makes clear that it is precisely his gospel that takes the righteousness of God seriously and, because it takes it seriously, sees humanity's plight as deeper than imagined and universal, requiring a radical solution that is for all.

4 Objections to and support for Paul's claim

Romans 3:1–20

In verses 1–8, Paul engages in a brief question-and-answer debate, anticipating the objections that a Jewish Christian dialogue partner will raise to his previous claims. The obvious objection is that any advantage from being a Jew has been completely annulled. In response, Paul embarks on a delicate balancing act, already hinted at in the earlier statements about 'all' that assign Jews a certain priority. Both salvation and judgement of deeds involve 'the Jew first and also the Greek' (1:16; 2:9–10). Here he is content to state that yes, Jewish ethnic identity still has significance in the outworking of God's purposes (v. 2), but no, ultimately Jew and Gentile are in the same position before God (v. 9). In regard to the first assertion, Paul gets only as far as listing one advantage—the scriptures have been entrusted to Israel—before being diverted by related questions, which at this stage are treated only cursorily. He postpones any detailed reply until later. Chapters 9—11 will take up the questions in verses 1–7 about Israel's advantages and Israel's faithlessness in relation to God's justice and faithfulness, while chapter 6 will answer the question in verse 8 about doing evil so that good may come.

Instead, Paul returns to his main claim that Jews are ultimately no better off because they are part of the 'all' who are 'under sin'. This different formulation reflects Paul's belief (again, to be developed in chapters 5—7) that sinning involves not only committing individual sins but also being under the dominion of sin as one of the powers of this age. The scriptures that form part of Israel's privileged priority in fact confirm his charge that Jews are equally enslaved to sin's pervasive and extensive rule. The response to his devastating chain of references, indicating that no one is righteous or seeks God, could well have been that his judgement must apply only to Gentiles or to apostate Jews. But Paul claims that what the law, in the form of scripture, says, it says to those who possess it. The modification of Septuagint Psalm 142:2 (143:2 in most English Bibles) and the addition of 'by deeds prescribed by the law' in verse 20 then provide an appropriate conclusion to this section's indictment of all humanity, which has specified that 'all' includes Jews.

5 God remains just while justifying

Romans 3:21–31

Now back to the good news—but with a greater appreciation of why it is so amazingly good. Simply put, it is that God's justice has been disclosed in a way that makes its positive verdict freely available to all humans. Since this verdict is received through faith, it is accessible to both Jews and Gentiles.

Justification as a gift to humans, despite what they deserve, does not mean that God's righteousness and accompanying condemnation of sinful humans have been set aside. On the contrary, what God has done in Christ enables God both to remain righteous and to justify the one who has faith in Jesus (v. 26). In showing how this can be, Paul employs three main images to depict what God accomplished in Jesus' death, and each matches a major element of the plight he has depicted.

* Justification is imagery from the law court. Failure to acknowledge the Creator had left humans without excuse and guilty, but God's justice is the power that sets them in a right relation with God, pronouncing a pardon for them so that their deserved guilt is no longer held against them.

- Redemption is imagery from the slave-market that also has its roots in God's liberation of Israel from slavery in Egypt. Humans' plight involved being in bondage to the power of sin, but God's justice emancipates them from this dominion.
- Atonement is sacrificial imagery that has both expiatory (making amends for sin) and propitiatory (averting divine wrath on account of sin) connotations. Paul could not have been clearer that all were under God's righteous wrath, but, in dealing with sin, Christ's atoning death also averts that wrath.

In verses 29–30 Paul appeals to the fundamental Jewish belief, confessed in the *Shema* (Deuteronomy 6:4), that God is one, and claims that the gospel of justification by faith is more appropriate to this universal monotheism than is an insistence on the law. There are not two routes to salvation, one by law (plus faith) and the other simply by faith. The one God is the same God of both Jews and Gentiles and acts in one and the same way towards both groups, demonstrating this unity of action by justifying the circumcised and the uncircumcised through the same faith.

6 Witness to the gospel and father of believers

Romans 4

Paul substantiates his claim of still upholding the law (3:31) by calling on Abraham as the law's witness (see 3:21) both to justification by faith (not works of the law, thus excluding boasting) and to faith as the unifying factor for Jewish Christians and Gentile Christians. Genesis 15:6, the key text for Paul's interpretation (vv. 3, 9, 22), states that Abraham was reckoned righteous by faith, without any mention of works. This enables Paul to press the point that there can be no thought of justification being owed to Abraham through his successfully passing a divine judgment according to his deeds (v. 4).

Paul emphasises especially the sequence of events in Genesis, showing that the statement in Genesis 15:6 comes before the account of Abraham's circumcision in Genesis 17. When Abraham was reckoned righteous by faith, he was still uncircumcised (vv. 9–10), putting him at this point in precisely the same position as the Gentile Christian. What is more, the promise about his inheritance was believed by Abraham before the law, anticipated in the requirement of circumcision, was given (vv. 13–15). This means that Abraham should be seen not just as 'our ancestor according to the flesh' (v. 1) but as the ancestor of all who believe—circumcised, law-observant Jewish Christians as well as Gentile Christians (vv. 11b–12, 16–17a). Paul's presentation of Abraham as a symbol of unity has clear implications for the tensions between Jewish and Gentile Christian readers in Rome, who need to see that sharing Abraham's justifying faith makes both groups equal members of the one family.

Genesis 15:6 still speaks (vv. 23–24), because Abraham's faith in the promise about his descendants was a belief in the God who raises the dead. Being placed in a right relationship with God is like Isaac coming to birth, despite Abraham being as good as dead and the deadness of Sarah's womb (v. 19). So Abraham becomes a type of Christian believers, whose justification is through belief in the God who raised Jesus from the dead, thereby reversing the condemnation of his death in a vindicating verdict, which also becomes theirs: he 'was raised for our justification' (v. 25). Justification, then, involves a radical intervention on God's part to rescue humanity from its situation of death and bring it into the realm of life.

Guidelines

For those of us who preach and teach, Paul's confidence about the good news of what God has done in the death and resurrection of Christ can prove a tonic. For him, proclamation is not about hawking one more piece of propaganda in the marketplace of ideas; it means pointing to the life-bringing power of God in Christ that is at the gospel's heart. This assures us that the effectiveness of our ministries does not ultimately depend on us, and it frees us to trust in the gospel's inherent power to unleash God's transforming justice into the world.

At the same time, Paul's articulation of the implications of the gospel contains concepts that some Christians find difficult or offensive. For example, some find no place for the wrath of God or a view of Christ's death as an atoning sacrifice that propitiates that wrath (3:24–26). They see the former as detracting from the affirmation that God is love and as making God capricious and vengeful. They tend to caricature the latter either as a loving Jesus wringing forgiveness from a hostile God or as a tyrannical God imposing violence on an innocent Son.

Both wrath and love in relation to God are, of course, analogies, containing both similarities and dissimilarities to the human qualities that the terms denote. But if we hold, for example, that the abuse and murder of children, genocide and the wanton destruction of the environment are evil, is a God who does not passionately condemn such actions and their agents worthy of our worship? God's love is not reducible to sentimentality but is a holy love. Seeing atonement as cosmic child abuse is to take metaphor literally and impose a division between Jesus and God that is foreign to Christian theology. In the wake of the human violence that produced Jesus' death, Paul can now see his death as a sign that the Father and the Son are at one in an act of love; this act constitutes God's self-giving in order to deal with the condemnation that sinful deeds rightly deserve (5:6–8).

Are divine wrath and divine love incompatible? Is the atonement metaphor too easily misunderstood to be useful or does it remain important as one of the models needed to begin to comprehend Christ's death? If we say that God's righteousness is just as accurately rendered as God's justice, does this shed light on the questions?

1 Living in hope and through a representative

Romans 5

If God has pronounced a positive verdict for believers ahead of the final judgement, where are the benefits that the Jews expected to follow such judgement—life, peace and glory? Do not suffering and death, in the present age, make this perspective illusory? Paul's response in verses 1–11 is that such benefits are already experienced in hope. Hope is not simply a wished-for possibility but an assured conviction, based on God's faithfulness to God's promises. Indeed, when sufferings are encountered in faith, they produce not embitterment or disillusionment but the endurance and character that strengthen hope. Hope is also grounded in the experience of God's love through the Spirit. If, through Christ's death, that profound love has already performed the unimaginably difficult task of justifying the guilty and reconciling those who were enemies of God, then there can be an assurance that God will accomplish the comparatively easy matter of completing the salvation that has been inaugurated (vv. 6–11).

Paul has repeatedly stated that the salvation under way is 'through our Lord Jesus Christ' (vv. 1–2, 9–11). But how can all benefit from the death and life of one man? Here Paul turns to the scriptural story of Adam for an analogy. That story can be interpreted as one man's misdeed having universal consequences in terms of sin and death. In line with the notion of representative solidarity found in the Jewish scriptures, whereby a whole group of people can be depicted as in solidarity with an ancestor or leader who represents them, Adam's sin can even be seen as the sin of all. Similarly, claims Paul, through God's grace all are constituted right or just by Christ's one act of obedience, and thereby experience justification and life (vv. 18–19). Since humans are in bondage to the system of sin and death, they cannot be restored on their own. God has to give what God requires, and God gives it through a representative.

However, the analogy with the story of Adam's sin also falls short. Whereas, through Adam, humans were in bondage under the dominion of death, in the new sphere, in which grace abounds or 'super-abounds', believers are not only subjects under a new power; they also share in its dominion through their representative, Christ, as they live out the life of the age to come (vv. 17b, 20b–21).

2 Living freed from sin

Romans 6

If there is an abundance of grace, and if the law that was meant to prevent sin is no longer decisive for a right relationship with God, does it mean that people can continue to sin with impunity? This same basic objection to Paul's gospel is formulated in two slightly different ways (vv. 1, 15). Two main arguments back his emphatic rejection of such thinking: believers have been freed from sin through their solidarity with Christ in his death to sin (vv. 2–14) and, having been freed from sin, they have become slaves of righteousness (vv. 16–23).

Shaping these arguments is a contrast between two different dominions, already described in the previous section as sin and death, on the one hand, and grace and justice, on the other (5:17, 21). 'Sin' now continues as the major term for the negative dominion, indicating that Paul's focus is not on individual acts of sinning but on sin personified as a power to which humans are subject. For the positive power, there is more variation in terminology: grace (vv. 14–15), obedience (v. 16), righteousness/justice (vv. 18–20) and God (vv. 10–13, 22–23).

Key to believers' identity is their baptism, through which they have been transferred from the old realm to the new. Baptism signifies their solidarity with Christ in his death and resurrection, which decisively ('once for all', v. 10) inaugurated a new world order within history. Through union with Christ's death and resurrection, the person who was aligned with the old dominion has been crucified and has died to sin, so that sin's hold is broken and he or she is made a new person who experiences 'newness of life' (v. 4b). Believers are summoned to recognise that this reality of what God accomplished in Christ establishes their identity: 'consider yourselves dead to sin and alive to God' (v. 11). Then, because as yet they are still in mortal bodies vulnerable to the influences of this age, believers are exhorted to live out their new identity by refusing to allow sin any further dominion (v. 13). They have come under a new power, but one that provides the freedom to place their bodies voluntarily at the disposal of God, to be employed as weapons of justice in the conflict resulting while the old order and the new still overlap (vv. 13–14, 19).

3 Living freed from the law

Romans 7

The law is the basis neither for justification nor for living justly. Identified with Christ's death, believers have in fact died to the law in order to become subject to a new power, now described as 'the new life of the Spirit' (vv. 1–6). It is not, Paul hastens to add, that Torah is the same as sin. After all, it is God's law and is good (vv. 7, 12–16, 22), yet it is limited in what it is able to achieve. Its commandments can indicate what is sinful but are unable to prevent a person from sinning. What is worse, operating in the old order of sin, such commandments actually provoke and arouse sin.

Verses 7–25 are among the most disputed sections of the New Testament. Who is the 'I' engaged in a hopeless struggle with the law? Some see these verses as autobiographical, with Paul depicting his own past, but this flies in the face of his statement elsewhere that he saw himself as blameless in regard to the law's just standard (see Philippians 3:6). Others think that Paul is describing the normal life of a believer, caught between lifelong frustration and eschatological hope. But this person says, 'I am of the flesh, sold into slavery under sin' (v. 14), whereas Paul has previously said that his readers *were* slaves to sin but are now freed (6:14, 20, 22) and will later say that they are *not* in the flesh but in the Spirit (8:9). The most coherent view is that Paul is employing the device of 'speech-in-character' to portray as graphically as possible the plight of the Jew under the law, as seen now from the vantage point of the solution that God has provided in Christ.

Faced with the law they love, Jews who are still under the power of sin find themselves incapable of doing the good and, instead, do what they hate. While this may sound not very different from a realistic view of Christian existence, Paul takes a much more robust stance about normal Christian living and sin. He holds that the desperate plight of the divided person has been resolved through Christ and, in his gratitude, blurts out the solution before completing his summary of the plight (7:25). He then goes on to elaborate on the solution (8:1–13).

4 Living according to the Spirit

Romans 8:1–13

What the law could not do (discussed vividly in 7:14–25), God has done, in Christ and through the Spirit. Thus, humans are freed from the old dominion, in which the law was caught up with the powers of sin and death, and the just requirement of the law, its central thrust of love for neighbour (see 13:8–10), is able to be fulfilled in believers.

The exposition of this claim is set in the continuing contrast between two dominions, this time designated as flesh and Spirit. These are not, as has sometimes been thought, two parts of the same person—the physical and sensual over against the inner and spiritual. When the word 'flesh' is employed with negative connotations, it refers not so much to finite physical life as to this life in its hostility to and alienation from God—the life of this present evil age. The Spirit refers to the divine Spirit, who in Jewish expectation would be poured out on humanity in the end-times, bringing resurrection life. The Spirit mediates the life and power of the age to come as its first fruits (8:23). For Paul, then, a person's whole self, including the mind and the body, is aligned either with the sphere of the flesh or with the sphere of the Spirit. In regard to the latter, the believer lives in the sphere of the Spirit and the Spirit's power but, at the same time, the Spirit (who can also be designated as the Spirit of God or the Spirit of Christ) lives in the believer (vv. 9–11).

The cryptic clause, 'the Spirit is life because of righteousness' (v. 10), calls to mind the letter's theme text: 'The one who by faith is righteous shall live' (1:17, author's translation). As noted in the comments on that text, in Jewish expectation the blessing of life in its fullness would follow on from God's verdict at the last judgement. Believers in Christ experience ahead of time the life of the Spirit, made available because of the just Judge's positive verdict. In the present overlap of the ages, the believer's body is still mortal until it too is given full resurrection life, yet the Spirit enables what is done in this body not to be determined by death's lingering encroachment but to display life: 'you will live' (vv. 10–13).

5 Living as heirs of God

Romans 8:14–39

This section of the argument about believers' experience of the life of the coming age now reaches a rhetorical climax. No more is needed than to pause and note the sequence of thought before rereading the passage for its spiritual force.

Paul has been clear that believers in Christ are subject to a new dominion but he is aware that slavery is a less than adequate image for this relationship (see, for example, 6:19). He now employs another image, that of adoption, from the Greco-Roman practice whereby a young male adult could be given legal rights to carry on a family's name and share its inheritance. The Spirit confirms that believers have been adopted as sons and daughters in God's family and, therefore, are heirs of God and joint-heirs with Christ. Their inheritance is described as 'glory' (vv. 17–18, 21, 30), the radiant divine presence that transforms both humanity (completing adoption with a resurrected body, v. 23) and the created cosmos (setting it free from futility and corruption, vv. 20–21).

Present sufferings constitute evidence for rather than against this hope of glory. They are part of the labour pains of the renewed creation, which is being delivered out of the womb of the old. Believers participate in a chorus of groans, as, in solidarity with the suffering of the rest of humanity and the creation as a whole, they cry out in painful longing for the glorified world to arrive (vv. 22–23). Sometimes, in their weakness, believers are unable to articulate their suffering and compassion, but, when words fail, the Spirit's own groaning turns the groans of believers into effective intercession.

All this is part of hope (vv. 24–25), and that hope of inheriting glory is assured because of God's sovereign call and God's secure love. What God has purposed is as good as done. If God has already called and justified believers, God has certainly glorified them (vv. 28–30). And if God's love was such as to give up the Son for us, there can be no doubt that, with him, God will 'give us everything else' (literally, 'all things'), including the promised glory (v. 32). If, in Christ, God has demonstrated that God is *for* us to this extent, that clearly settles the matter of the full inheritance. Who or what, of sufficient significance, could be against us or separate us from such a love?

6 What of God's faithful justice towards Israel?

Romans 9:1–29

This new section of the letter is no digression. Having just rejoiced in the assured benefits of adoption and glory for believers in Christ, Paul faces with anguish the natural question, already broached in 3:1 and 9, of how Israel fits into this picture. His wish, if it were possible, to be cut off from

Christ for the sake of his own people, the Jews, indicates his belief that the majority of them are missing out on the benefits he has described. This is all the more tragic since, among the privileges that belong to Israel, sonship and glory are at the start of Paul's list, and the Messiah, in whom they should have believed, ends it (vv. 4–5). This situation raises a question about God. Paul has just insisted that God will assuredly carry out the divine purposes for believers, but how can this God be trusted if the divine promises for Israel are not fulfilled? Paul wrestles with this issue in various ways throughout chapters 9—11, seeking illumination from and frequently citing his Jewish scriptures.

He begins by insisting that God's promise to Abraham has not failed because it was never made to all ethnic Israelites anyway. As in Galatians 4:21–31, he claims that there has always been a distinction between the 'children of the promise', such as Isaac and Jacob, and the 'children of the flesh', because God has discriminated not on the basis of individuals' works but simply on the basis of God's call (vv. 6–16). This is not unjust, since no human could earn God's call. The sovereign God can show mercy to or harden the heart of whomever God wills, in order to accomplish God's universal purposes (vv. 14–18).

In the face of this sovereignty, though, how can humans be held accountable? Employing the scriptural image of God as the potter, Paul compares the posing of such a question to a pot disputing with its creator about the purpose for which it has been made. In creating different groups out of the same people, God might have purposes that contribute to God's glory and the glory of those to whom mercy is shown. God's promises have not failed, because those prepared for glory include both ethnic Jews (Isaiah 10:22–23 prophesies about the remnant within Israel) and Gentiles (Hosea speaks of those who were not God's people becoming children of the living God).

Guidelines

For Paul, there are two dominions or power spheres, and humans live in one or the other. On the one side there is sin and the flesh, accompanied by idolatry, the law and death, while on the other there is God and the Spirit, accompanied by life, freedom and love.

Some present-day readers may not easily relate to the notion that we live subject to a power. A person's autonomy or freedom is frequently stressed and we talk constantly of exercising choice. Yet we also know that our lives are conditioned by a variety of forces over which we have no control: we talk about those who live subject to fashion or under the control of an addiction. Similarly, when Paul talks of idolatry (1:23–25) as a major aspect of sin's dominion, he means that the centre of one's life is something that cannot bear the weight—some aspect of created reality rather than the Creator. Whether it is another person, work, family, sex or physical fitness, this centre of power has to be maintained by unceasing effort, resulting in compulsion (another term for enslavement) and the distortion of other relationships.

For Paul, the events of Christ's death and resurrection are the medium of God's grace, which breaks the hold of the old syndrome of enslavement and death. Baptism is the symbol of believers' participation in these events, whereby through faith they are decisively realigned with the Creator as the centre of power and transferred to the new and liberating sphere of God's Spirit and life (6:3–11; 8:2–11). This centre now establishes our identity, and we need continually to recall who we now are and what is our new centre of power—the Spirit of Christ within us. In appropriating these enabling resources, we discover that this new dominion is one where, in the words of the Book of Common Prayer, 'service is perfect freedom'.

Spend some time meditating and praying about what it means for your past, present and future that absolutely nothing can separate you from the love of God in Christ Jesus (8:35–39).

1 Israel's culpability

Romans 9:30—10:21

Why is it that Gentiles who were not seeking God's justice have attained it through faith, while the Israelites, who pursued it zealously, have missed out? Paul's answer builds on the conviction that the solution to the human plight is through justification by faith. Israel's zeal has to be seen as misguided because it sought God's justice on the basis of the law and therefore of performance. This route was a cul-de-sac, as 2:12–29 has already demonstrated. Paul now combines Isaiah 8:14 and 28:16 to claim that when God sent the Messiah as a cornerstone on which to build in faith, Israel instead tripped over it as a stumbling-stone (9:33). Israel failed to recognise that Christ is the end of the law, bringing to a close its era along with any attempted route to God's saving justice on its basis, and opening up a new route for all, both Jews and Gentiles, by means of faith (10:4).

The contrast between these two routes, Paul claims, is already present in the Torah. On the one hand, Leviticus 18:5 sets out the law's principle that justification and life are on the basis of doing (10:5), while, on the other, Deuteronomy 30:12–14 shows the way of faith (vv. 6–8). In its original context, the latter text asserted that keeping the law is not something too hard or inaccessible! Because he is convinced that Christ is the end of the law, Paul, in citing this text, omits its words about doing and replaces the role of Torah with that of Christ. This scripture now speaks of the accessibility and ease of faith in Christ. Nothing impossible is required, simply confessing with the lips that Jesus is Lord and believing in the heart that God raised him from the dead (vv. 5–10).

This gospel may be accessible but, if there is to be faith, it needs to be heard. Paul insists that everything necessary for hearing has already occurred but has not led to faith on Israel's part (vv. 14–18). The only explanation left—that somehow Israel did not understand the message—is ruled out. It cannot be that Israel is more foolish than the foolish Gentiles who have grasped it (see Deuteronomy 32:21). Instead, the indictment in Isaiah 65:2 must apply (v. 21). In its rejection of the good news, Israel is a disobedient people and without excuse.

2 God's irrevocable calling of Israel

Romans 11

For Paul, Israel's present disobedience in relation to the good news of its Messiah is not the last word and certainly does not entail that God has rejected Israel. God has frequently worked through a remnant as a pledge of what God will do for the whole nation, and at present there is a remnant of ethnic Jews, chosen by grace, of whom Paul is a representative (vv. 1–5). The hardening and stumbling of the rest of Israel have turned out to be a blessing for the Gentiles, to whom the good news has now spread, and Paul sees his own apostleship to the Gentiles as part of God's purposes to make Israel jealous. A note of hopefulness begins to sound, as Paul considers that if God can produce good from Israel's unbelief and its present reduction to a remnant, then, through Israel's acceptance of the Messiah and through its full number God will bring about the general resurrection of the dead as the climax of God's purposes (vv. 11–16).

Paul is addressing those Gentile Christians who may boast that they have simply replaced Israel in God's plan. His allegory of the olive tree is directed against any such presumption. If God could perform the miracle of grafting Gentiles as wild olive shoots into the domestic olive tree, how much more likely that God will be able to take the broken natural branches, Jews who failed to believe, and graft them back into their own tree (vv. 17–24). Indeed, the 'mystery', the divine plan now revealed in Christ, is that the present hardening of the majority of Israel will be only until the Gentile mission reaches its fulfilment, and this will inaugurate the salvation of 'all Israel'. Israel, in this phrase, retains the ethnic meaning that it has had in the discussion to this point and is not, as some have argued, a reference to all believers as a spiritual Israel. Ethnic Israel as a whole will receive God's mercy through the deliverer, Christ, and in this way God's mercy will be shown to all, both ethnic Jews and ethnic Gentiles (vv. 25–32).

This whole section, which started as a lament over Israel, concludes with a doxology to the God into whose inscrutable ways Paul believes he has caught a glimpse (vv. 33–36).

3 The justice and mercy of God

Romans 12

The 'therefore' in verse 1 should be taken seriously. The exhortations in 12:1—15:13 have their basis in the whole of Paul's preceding rehearsal of his gospel. The argument about the saving justice of God, the resulting new life and the overwhelming mercy of God for both Jews and Gentiles has climaxed in a doxology; all that remains is that such a response of praise and worship should be fleshed out in the believers' communal living. Paul's exhortations also advance his mission, whose goal is to bring about 'the obedience of faith' (1:5) or to ensure that the Gentiles' offering to God is 'acceptable, sanctified by the Holy Spirit' (15:15–16). The specific situation of the recipients will be addressed directly in 14:1—15:13, but the preceding more general exhortations already have an eye on the conflict between the weak and strong in faith. Having a sober estimate of one's own measure of faith (v. 3), appreciating the diversity in the one body (vv. 4–8), demonstrating love and mutual affection (vv. 9–10) and living in harmony with one another (v. 16) are all behaviours that would change the dynamics of the relationships between the groups in Rome.

It is worth dwelling briefly on the way Paul introduces this section (vv. 1–2). Previously, worship, including the sacrificial rituals, had been listed as among Israel's privileges (9:4). Now the sacrificial worship that Paul urges on believers as 'reasonable', as the only appropriate response to the gospel, is the presentation of their whole embodied selves to God as an offering. The sacrifice is 'living' not simply because, in contrast to other sacrifices, it has not been killed, but because it shares the quality of the new life (compare 6:13: 'present yourselves to God as those who have been brought from death to life'). Paul's contrast between two dominions has been variously formulated. Here the underlying contrast between two ages becomes explicit. 'Do not be conformed to this age' presupposes that believers already participate in the age to come and are therefore able to resist the insidious pressures of the old order's values by allowing the powers of the new order to continue to transform them. This process involves a continuous renewal of the mind, which enables the believing community to discern and test what is ethically appropriate in the situations it faces.

4 Relating to the governing authorities

Romans 13

Paul has already advised that the letter's recipients should live peaceably with all (12:18), and he now contributes to their discernment of what is good in relation to the governing authorities (vv. 3–4) by urging them to pay their taxes (vv. 6–7). The preceding theological support for this specific exhortation is drawn from traditional Jewish wisdom, which taught that the state takes its authority from and is accountable to God in order to promote the common good as a servant of God.

Two sorts of tax are mentioned in verse 7—a direct tax collected by government officials and an indirect tax, including export and import duties, collected by the Roman military police. The latter was causing unrest because it was often subject to corruption. But withholding taxes was also the first sign of a people's rebellion against the state, and Paul does not want the Roman Christians to give this signal. Just a few years before, in AD49, Claudius had expelled Jewish Christians, along with other Jews, from Rome because of rioting that occurred among Jews in connection with proclamation of the gospel. Paul judges that avoidance of the tax issue is also more likely to produce the social stability that will aid in strengthening relations between the house churches in Rome. He therefore calls on those Jews who have now returned to Rome, and on the Gentile Christian majority, to honour the powers-that-be by paying both kinds of tax.

If what is owed to the state authorities is the payment of taxes, what is owed to others is love, an obligation without limits. In loving their neighbour, which summarises the law, the community is in fact fulfilling the law (vv. 8–10). As Paul has explained in 8:4, this fulfilment now takes place through the Spirit, as believers align themselves with this power of the new age. That new order, depicted through the images of the day and the light, has broken into the night and darkness of the old order. Since the full day will soon arrive, believers' appropriation of the new order is all the more urgent and can be seen as living in the day, putting on the armour of light or simply putting on the Lord Jesus Christ, whose death and resurrection define its quality of life.

5   Unity in diversity for the sake of God's glory

Romans 14:1—15:13

Tᵀˢ exhortations come to a climax as Paul addresses issues that have
between the self-styled 'strong in faith', the predominantly Gentian majority, and the predominantly Jewish Christians whom

they dub the 'weak in faith'. The latter hold that their obedience to God demands that they eat only vegetables and keep certain days holy, and they are not happy with those who boast that their strong faith permits them to consider all foods clean (on the basis that, in Christ, nothing is unclean in itself) and no day more or less sacred.

Paul is not interested here in arguing for a particular position, although he indicates that he shares the viewpoint of the strong (15:1). What troubles him is the attitude of both groups: the weak are judging and the strong are despising those who are their brothers and sisters (14:3–4, 10, 13). So his appeal is for unity despite their theological and ethical differences. It now becomes clear how his rehearsal of the gospel in terms of Jews and Gentiles being one and equal has a direct bearing on the problems of the house churches in Rome. The second clause in the key summarising exhortation—'Welcome one another, therefore, just as Christ has welcomed you' (15:7)—is a reminder of their justification by God through Christ. If the divine verdict is what counts, there can be no room for despising and judging one another. Each is accountable to God and Christ (14:4, 7–12).

In this way Paul expects believers to live in harmony with those whose views they find deficient, respecting the integrity of others' motives and their desire to honour their Lord (14:5–6), and not imposing their own norms on those who have not internalised them (14:15, 20–23). He wants God to get the glory from the existence of the different Christian groups in Rome as they become a worshipping community that, together and with one voice, glorifies the God and Father of the Lord Jesus Christ (15:6). In a powerful conclusion, demonstrating that division must give way to doxology, Paul draws on the words of scripture to reinforce his belief that Jews and Gentiles are woven together in God's redemptive plan in the Messiah. Thus he calls on Jews to praise God among the Gentiles and Gentiles to rejoice with God's people, the Jews (15:8–13).

6 Paul's mission and co-workers

Romans 15:14—16:27

In the letter's address to the Roman Christians (1:7), Paul does not use the term 'church'. We now find in 16:3–15, though, that he greets different groups attached to particular leaders and households. These house churches in Rome are likely to have come into existence at various times and with varying conceptions of the implications of the gospel.

In this section, despite what is said in other Pauline letters about their restricted role in his churches, women have a prominent place among Paul's co-workers. So we find, for example, the commendation of Phoebe (the probable bearer of the letter) as a deacon, the mention of Prisca before her husband Aquila, and the description of Junia as 'prominent among the apostles'.

Earlier in the letter's closing section, Paul talks of his role as apostle to the Gentiles and of his travel plans (15:14–33). Here it becomes clear that he perceives his mission as worldwide, encompassing the extent of Rome's empire. He believes that he has accomplished his pioneering mission in the east (15:19) by seeing firmly settled churches in progress in the various provinces. It now remains for him to move on to the west, to Spain, which, in the geography of his day, was described as the western extremity of the inhabited world. This letter is a crucial part of his plan, because he intends to go by way of Rome and needs the unified backing of its Christians (15:23–24, 28–29, 32).

One prior item on Paul's agenda, however, would crown his mission in the east—his impending visit to Jerusalem, accompanied by delegates from the churches of the Gentile mission, with the collection, whose receipt would be a sign of the unity of the early Christian movement (15:25–28). Yet this outcome is not a foregone conclusion, because acceptance of financial relief by the strongly Jewish-Christian Jerusalem church would also signal acceptance of his Gentile mission, with its law-free gospel. He therefore asks the Roman Christians to support this part of his mission also through their earnest prayers for its success (15:30–31). Clearly the tensions between Gentile Christians and Jewish Christians, both in his own mission as a whole and in Rome, have had a bearing on this letter's rehearsal of his gospel of God's grace in Christ for all, the Jew first and also the Gentile.

Guidelines

Romans 14:1—15:13 indicates particularly clearly how Paul's theological exposition of the good news of God's saving justice is meant to affect personal and corporate living. Paul's vision is of a new community of justice and love that will transcend the major division in his first-century world—that between Jews and Gentiles. It will be made possible if they all heed his exhortation: 'Welcome or accept one another, as Christ has welcomed or accepted you' (see 15:7). The justification language, with its forensic connotations of pardon and vindication on the basis of God's grace in Christ, is translated into the more personal idiom of Christ's acceptance of people. Christ's acceptance of Jewish and Gentile believers, purely through grace, means that both groups can now accept one another.

How far do our own churches, in their structures, teaching and life, demonstrate the possibility of overcoming gender, sexual, ethnic, social and economic divisions? And how do they handle theological and ethical differences about how the gospel is to make this demonstration?

Any response to such questions requires us to keep on returning to the basis of Paul's vision and pondering whether we are really convinced that God has justified us and Christ has accepted us just as we are. When this good news grasps us, we can relax and abandon our own projects for acceptance from some other source, because we are accepted at the heart of reality, with all our vulnerability and our failure to live justly and lovingly. We are then set free to accept others, to let others in the community be who they are—with their different backgrounds, viewpoints and vulnerabilities.

When Paul called for this accepting love, the differences he made room for were not over trivial details of interpretation or practice but over the fundamental issue of whether God's will as revealed in Torah had continuing validity. The 'strong' believers were asked to remain in communion with those who held views that they considered insufficiently impacted by the gospel; similarly, the 'weak' needed to remain in unity with those who were doing things they deemed morally offensive to God. When a disposition of love, on the basis of Christ's acceptance, replaces scorn and judgement, it becomes possible for 'traditionalists' and 'progressives' to live and worship together.

In the midst of our present dispiriting divisions, it is the Spirit of the God of hope who enables us to abound in hope (15:13), to keep alive this vision of a pluralistic communion and to risk the practice of accepting love, in anticipation of a future renewal of which our present fragmentary experiences are only a sign.

FURTHER READING

Douglas J. Moo, *Encountering the Book of Romans* (2nd edn), Baker Academic, 2014.

A. Katherine Grieb, *The Story of Romans*, Westminster John Knox, 2002.

James D.G. Dunn, *Romans* (Word Biblical Commentary, 2 Vols.), Word, 1988.

N. Thomas Wright, 'The Letter to the Romans' in *New Interpreter's Bible* Vol. X, Abingdon Press, 2002, pp. 393–770.

Robert Jewett, *Romans* (Hermeneia), Fortress, 2007.

Incarnation (Part 1)

For me, as a Baptist, singing is a rather special aspect of Christmas. We Baptists have little or no set liturgy, so singing is the main form of collective participation in our worship, and Christmas is marked more than any other season by a wonderful set of songs. From the first strains of 'O come, O come, Emmanuel', as Advent begins, to the climax of 'Yes, Lord, we greet thee...' on Christmas morning, the songs mark the season out.

The songs and other events of Christmas celebrate the incarnation—God become human, God come among us as one of us. In the classic carol service we mark it with a festival of lessons and carols, readings carefully selected to suggest that the incarnation was always inevitable, and songs that celebrate the fact. As we will see, however, even if God's coming is obvious to us in retrospect, in prospect it was, at the very least, obscure. The event of incarnation might *make sense* of all the prophecies that came before, but it was not clearly *predicted* in them.

Jesus is both truly human, a human being like you and me, and God present with us. This is the astonishing truth of the incarnation. We can get this wrong in two different ways: we can stress the human, and not see God's presence in Jesus, or we can stress the divine, and not see that Jesus is just as human as we are. Over the next week we will look at scriptures that prefigure the incarnation, scriptures that explain it, and scriptures that presume it. We will see how the Bible constructs this truth, and what difference it makes to us.

Direct quotations are taken from the New International Version of the Bible.

14–20 December

1 Being human

Genesis 2:4–25

If we are trying to understand what it means for God to become human, we have to begin by asking what it means to be human. The Bible gives us two stories of creation in the beginning; in the first, found in Genesis

1:1—2:3, we have a beautiful poem structured around seven days, with human beings appearing as the pinnacle of creation, made in the image of God. Genesis 2 gives us the second story. Humanity still has a special place in the created order in this story: the whole narrative is structured around the creation of human beings and God's provision of a world for them to live in.

In this story, however, the stress is on the physicality of being human. To be human means to be made from the dust of the ground, to do physical labour in the garden, to need to eat (and to find pleasure in eating), and to find fulfilment in physical and sexual relationships. To be human is to be bound up with blood and mud and dirt and juice and flesh.

When we speak of God becoming human, this is what we mean. God entered our world of mess and dirt and dust and flesh. God embraced it and became a part of it. We sometimes talk of religion in terms of 'spirituality', which can sound as if we are dealing with a realm opposed to the physical and corporal. Christian spirituality must always be totally physical, totally corporeal, because in Jesus God becomes totally physical, totally corporeal.

Of course, we know this. We structure our spiritual lives around an initial act of washing, in baptism, and a repeated act of eating, in Holy Communion. But we sometimes make both acts so symbolic, so abstracted from real washing and real eating, that we can lose the connection. Because a morsel of bread and a sip of wine is so much less corporeal than a still-bleeding steak, we tend to believe that spirituality can and should be abstracted from the physical realm. Not if we believe in and follow Jesus, it shouldn't!

2 A hint of incarnation

Joshua 5:13—6:5

The story of Joshua at Jericho is well known; the repetitive marching and trumpet blasts make it a favourite with those who seek attractive stories for children. It starts and ends with more disturbing or confusing passages, however. At the end, as so often in Joshua, there is a horrific act of slaughter and destruction, apparently performed in obedience to divine command, and at the start we find this story of Joshua's encounter with God.

Joshua meets a 'man' (5:13) who identifies himself as the 'commander of the army of the Lord' (v. 14). When the man speaks again, however, the text identifies him unambiguously as 'the Lord' (6:2), and he gives Joshua instructions for overcoming the city. This pattern, in which a man appears and is then identified as God when he speaks, occurs more than once in the early books of the Bible (in addition to Genesis 18, where it is actually three men, see Genesis 32:24–30, where Jacob meets a man but finds that he has wrestled with God).

A very early Christian writer, Irenaeus, read these passages and suggested that the divine Son was so eager to take on human form that he could not wait for the appointed moment, and kept appearing as a human being through Israel's history. This idea might seem rather fanciful, though beautiful. Yet today's text does suggest something like it: Joshua saw 'a man'—not 'something that looked like a man', not 'an angel in human shape', but 'a man'—and that man was God. With nothing more than this passage in Joshua, we might ignore the detail; knowing what we know of God's purposes, though, we perhaps should pay attention to it.

There is one other thing to notice: Joshua, setting out to conquer the land by war, naturally asks of a man with a sword, 'Whose side are you on?' (see 5:13). The answer is startling. Joshua has been given God's command to fulfil the promise of the exodus by conquering Canaan; if ever a military commander could claim to have 'God on his side', it was him. God, however, will not take sides, even in this war. 'Neither,' he replies; 'but as commander of the army of the Lord I have now come' (v. 14). Joshua is called to be on God's side, not to claim that God is on his. The distinction is very important.

3 King and priest

Psalm 110

Yesterday we saw the merest hint of a coming incarnation in the text of Joshua; it is hard to find a stronger prediction anywhere else in the Hebrew scriptures. What we do find elsewhere, however, is a strengthening vision that God's purposes are wrapped up with the Davidic king—a vision that sometimes seems to require the king to be far more than merely human. Psalm 110 is a classic example.

The psalm has two divine pronouncements (vv. 1, 4), each followed by brief commentary. It begins with 'The Lord says' or 'An oracle of the Lord', a common way of introducing God's declarations in the prophets, but used only here in the psalms. If we imagine the oracle being spoken by a priest or prophet in the temple, then 'my lord' in verse 1 becomes nothing more than an honorific. The whole is a promise that the power of the king, here pictured largely in military terms (vv. 2–3), is guaranteed by God.

The last line of verse 3 is hard to translate. The most natural reading seems to promise eternal renewal to the king—something like 'like dew, your youth will come to you', suggesting a renewal of the king's vigour every morning. To most readers, this seems a sufficiently implausible promise that they find other interpretations. However, the second divine oracle seems to pick up that meaning: not only is the king a priest but he is a priest 'for ever' (v. 4). The 'order of Melchizedek' refers to Genesis 14:18–20, where Abraham meets a king named Melchizedek, who is also a priest of God. Israel's king, being a descendant of David (of the tribe of Judah), could not serve as a normal priest, since priests had to be descended from Levi's tribe. Verses 5–6 return to the theme of military success, while verse 7 returns to the idea of constant renewal.

Jesus quotes verse 1 (Luke 20:42–43); indeed, no other line from the psalms is mentioned more often in the New Testament. If the speaker of the psalm is David, then who is David's 'lord'? He must be a promised Messiah. Hebrews 7:11–22 makes a similar point about verse 4 and Jesus' priesthood. The psalm, with its promises of everlasting reign, seems to strain the possibilities of human kingship to breaking point, but the New Testament writers find in that tension a prophecy of the incarnation.

4 God's purposes in the birth of a child

Luke 1:26–38

Luke's stories of the birth of Jesus are full of theological import. Here, the angel tells Mary who Jesus will be, and draws on imagery and titles from the psalms and elsewhere to give concrete shape to the various messianic expectations that had grown up. Jesus is David's son and will be called 'Son of the Most High' (v. 32), a title that was used in the psalms for the kings of David's line (see, for example, Psalm 2:7; 89:26–27).

As we saw in Psalm 110 yesterday, however, the possibilities of normal kingship are being stretched by Gabriel's words: Jesus' reign will be endless, eternal (v. 33). The great sign of this in Luke's story is the miraculous nature of Jesus' birth: Mary, although a virgin, will become pregnant by the power of the Holy Spirit.

In Luke's stories we find a strong affirmation of the true humanity of Jesus. He is located in a human family, linked to the history of God's people and born of a human mother. Notice that the angel speaks of 'his father David' in verse 32, although we have only been told that Joseph, not Mary, is a descendant of David (v. 27); clearly, despite the intervention of the Spirit and the virgin birth, Joseph is to be regarded as Jesus' father.

On the other hand, Luke repeats insistently that this birth is not like any other, that God is intimately involved in it, and that the child born will stand in a unique relationship to God. There is no straightforward claim here that the child to be born will be God come in the flesh, no clear affirmation of the incarnation. There is, though, a conviction that God's purposes are wrapped up with the life of this child, as well as hints, as we have seen, that the work God is sending him to do is beyond the capabilities of any human person, particularly in its eternal nature.

5 Word made flesh

John 1:1–18

The beginning of John's Gospel gives us the clearest statement of incarnation found anywhere in the Gospels. The majestic poetry of the prologue tells us of the eternal existence, deity and significance of the Word, and of his role in creation; it ends with the revelation that in Jesus we meet this Word, become flesh.

The first five verses assert the deity of the Word, both directly ('the Word was God', v. 1) and by ascribing to him divine actions (creation) and attributes (eternity; possession of life). At the same time, a distinction is made: the Word was 'with' God and creation came 'through' the Word.

This paradox of identity and distinction is right at the heart of what eventually became the doctrine of the Trinity.

Verses 9–13 move on to the place of the Word in the world. Although he is the world's creator, he is unrecognised and rejected by it—but he brings salvation to anyone who does recognise and does not reject him.

Despite this exalted status—one with the eternal God, the creator, the redeemer—it seems as if the glory of the Word was invisible until the incarnation. Only when the Word became flesh could we actually see how wonderful and awesome he is (v. 14). In his incarnate state, he has given us abounding grace and truth. The prologue ends where it began, with the unity and distinction of the Father and the Son, or God and the Word, and with the promise of revelation through him.

The poetic form of the prologue is broken twice (vv. 6–8, 15) with glimpses of the story of John the Baptist. There is a definite shift of the tone of the language here, like prose breaking into poetry; it can be felt in the English translations, but is very obvious in the Greek. In both interpolations, John's place is to testify to the Word, to point to Jesus.

If the poetic prologue describes the great truths of eternity and salvation history, the introduction of John the Baptist grounds them in history. The incarnation is not an awesome myth but something that happened at an identifiable time and place, something that the Gospel writer, also called John, saw and is called to testify to. This is incarnation—the in-breaking of eternity into history; the coming of God into a normal human story. The Gospel's shifts of language illustrate the profound truth that its words describe.

6 One with the Father

John 10:22–38

With the opening question of this story, we are back to the messianic speculation that we saw in Psalm 110 and Luke 20. 'Tell us if you are the Messiah,' they demand (see v. 24). Jesus' response is slightly puzzling: nowhere in the Gospel (other than in private conversation with the woman at the well) has he told anyone that he is the Messiah, but presumably he means that his words and actions ought to have made the matter clear (verse 38 might hint at this). In any case, he says, knowledge of who he is comes only to those who are saved, those who are given to Jesus by the Father and kept safe. This leads us into another reflection on the relationship of Jesus to the Father.

We have five direct claims from Jesus: 'I and the Father are one' (v. 30); God chose Jesus and sent him (v. 36); 'I am God's Son' (v. 36); 'I do the works of my Father' (v. 37); and 'The Father is in me, and I in the Father' (v. 38). At the beginning and end of this list, again we have direct claims to identity with God, but in between we have the suggestion of distinction from God. Jesus does not explain how these two relate to each other, but it is obvious that his hearers think he is claiming to be God and are scandalised by the claim (although it seems likely that they have come looking for something to be scandalised by).

Jesus is one with the Father, the Son of the Father, and they enjoy a relationship of mutual indwelling (v. 38), the closest relationship imaginable. At the same time, Jesus is the one whom the Father chose and sent to do his works, to bring salvation to the world (the context of the phrase 'do the works of my Father' in verse 37 is all about salvation). Along with the relationship of identity and unity, there is an order to their relationship, suggested in the language of sonship: the Father sends and Jesus comes; the Father begins and Jesus carries forward. God's Son has come among us, as one of us, to bring us back to God: that is the heart of the mystery of the incarnation, and this is the great purpose of God the Father.

Guidelines

For ancient Israel, as perhaps for every culture, God was distant and feared. When they met God, the distance and fear only seemed to increase: Moses spoke to God on the mountain, but the command for everyone else was not to let even an animal wander on the slopes, or it would die (Exodus 19). God is awesome and unapproachable.

This is why the claim of the incarnation is so astonishing. If God is unapproachable, how can Mary carry God in her womb? Yet the church has insisted that she did, calling her *theotokos*, 'God-carrier', or *mater Dei*, 'mother of God'.

The problem turns around in the New Testament: Jesus is obviously a human being, obviously Mary's son, but can he really be God? The texts—including his own words—insist that, yes, he is. He is God come among us, God born as one of us, God sharing our experience of life.

With Christmas now only a few days away, we pause to consider Luke's account of the nativity. The week after, we will continue our study of the incarnation, examining what it means to say that Jesus is truly human. We will look at all the ways in which Jesus shares our experience. Meanwhile, we can give thanks that God is always with us, that our God has chosen to become one of us.

Luke 1—2

This week's reading not only serves to introduce us to Luke's Gospel, ready for next year, when it will feature as the lectionary Gospel, but it also provides us with our Advent preparation. These two chapters offer pen portraits of some of the best-loved Jewish characters in all the Gospels (Zechariah and Elizabeth, Mary and Joseph, Simeon and Anna), and they lay the foundations for the ministry of John the Baptist and, above all, the mission of Jesus. They also contain some of the best-known songs or prayers from the New Testament and, pre-eminently, the text that forms the basis of our construction of the Christmas Day events. Here we find the angels, the shepherds and the manger, echoed and elaborated in so many Christmas carols.

Luke's Gospel begins, of course, with a carefully constructed account of his role as a Gospel writer (1:1–4), in which he emphasises his function as a verifier of historical truth. We will consider this role as we start next year's notes, which will take us through the first 13 chapters of this wonderful book. It is equally true that Luke is a purveyor of truth, and he does this with profound skill as a writer.

As I have re-read the early chapters of Luke in preparation for writing these notes, I have become keenly aware of their role in preparing the way for the revelation of the story of Jesus, which will follow. Through these two chapters, Luke is sensitising and alerting us so that we are in the best possible place to receive the truth of the story he is about to recount. While our readings will cover these two chapters sequentially, the notes will seek to illuminate some of his 'techniques', which flow through the narrative. Look out for themes such as long-awaited promises fulfilled, increased divine–human activity, joyful and eager responses to God, the intensity of positive human emotions, surprise and even fear, heart- and mind-searching, and enthusiasm to share what has been discovered. All these traits, and more, generate a keen anticipation and openness to the mission of Jesus which is to come. We end up feeling, 'I can't wait to find out...'.

Quotations are taken from the New Revised Standard Version unless otherwise indicated.

1 Waiting

Luke 1:1–10

Luke's introduction makes it clear that something significant has happened. There are many who are eyewitnesses of it; accounts of this important event have been handed down and he has carefully investigated everything. But Luke appears to be something of a tease, for he does not name names. Unlike Mark, who gets straight on with it from verse 1 ('The beginning of the good news of Jesus Christ'), and Matthew, who immediately announces the genealogy of Jesus Christ, Luke gives nothing away. Luke keeps us waiting.

Advent is the formal time in the church year for waiting—the time when we remind ourselves of the various strata that are involved in forming the landscape of Christian theology and practice. Christian faith is not about aimless or vacuous waiting, though: we are awaiting something or someone. So the prophets provide an impression of the one who is to come, as well as generating a forward momentum of expectation, and John the Baptist increases that momentum. Then there is an appeal to us, in many New Testament scriptures, to live appropriately as those who recognise that darkness is not ultimate but is passing away, because the Christ who came is also the Christ who is to come. His birth was no false dawn.

Our first passage from Luke reminds us that there are many other kinds of personal waiting. For Zechariah and Elizabeth, there had been the endless daily, monthly, yearly wait for the good news that she had conceived. The pain of childlessness would have been intensified by the knowledge that their lack of a son meant that the holy line of Aaron would be weakened. Both Elizabeth and Zechariah were from the Aaronic line, as Luke emphasises (v. 5). As Zechariah went to perform the holy and highly significant role of burning incense in the temple, he was aware that he would never have a son to follow in his footsteps. In one sense, the waiting was over for them. They had gone on living righteously, which is an immense testimony to their faithfulness and integrity, but they had given up living in hope: 'Elizabeth was barren, and both were getting on in years' (v. 7).

Advent calls Christians to keep on waiting expectantly, even if the fulfilment takes decades or centuries. Such waiting requires integrity of lifestyle but also an active hope.

2 The angel and Zechariah

Luke 1:11–25

Zechariah may have been going about his priestly business, seeking to establish communication between God and his people, but, when God actually made himself known through an angel, he was 'gripped with fear' (v. 12, NIV). This describes an emotional response to an unexpected and even terrifying event, and it is the normal and appropriate response to the presence of the divine, particularly the visible presence, encountered other than in a dream or a vision (see also Exodus 3:5–6; Daniel 8:15–18; Luke 24:1–5, 36–37). If Zechariah had not responded in this way, it would have indicated that he didn't understand that it was God making himself known—and it might have excused his subsequent doubts and questions.

Equally normal is the initial response of the angel: 'Do not be afraid' (v. 13; see 2:9–10; John 6:20). The statement 'Your prayer has been heard' both reassures Zechariah and prepares him for the content of God's message. Zechariah hears not only that he and Elizabeth will have a son, but also that this will be a very special son indeed.

So far, so good! But not for much longer. Zechariah doubts and questions the message and so casts aspersions on the messenger. Now, for the first time, the angel reveals who he is: 'I am Gabriel' (v. 19). Usually, in the Bible, angels remain anonymous: their function is to convey divine messages, initiate divine actions and bring assistance to the person they address. However, during the centuries around the birth of Jesus, an interest in angels had increased, so their position in the hierarchies and their names had become more significant. Gabriel was one of God's foremost emissaries, which underlines the significance of his message and the serious consequences, for Zechariah, of doubting him.

Zechariah suffers the indignity of losing his ability to speak (and, possibly, hear as well). All he can do is wait for the fulfilment of God's promise.

3 The angel and Mary

Luke 1:26–38

Mary's encounter with the angel Gabriel is rather different from Zechariah's, and it is not only her encounter but also the way in which the account is presented that is different. Whereas Zechariah's angelic experience is described as taking place in the middle of his priestly activities, Gabriel's visit is announced right at the start of Mary's story. In Zechariah's case, the angel first 'appears', whereas with Mary we are told straight away that he is sent by God (compare verses 11 and 26). With Zechariah, the angel is anonymous, both for the reader and for Zechariah, until he pronounces his name to emphasise his authority. With Mary, the reader now knows who the angel is (and how he can react if provoked), but Gabriel never reveals his name to Mary. We are told of Zechariah's fear response at the moment when the angel appears (v. 12), whereas Mary is first addressed in those famous words, 'Greetings, you who are highly favoured! The Lord is with you' (v. 28, NIV). She responds with anxiety to the angel's words, not his appearance.

Do these variations indicate a difference in the purpose, origin or genre of the narratives? Are they intended to provide artistic variety, or are they purely accidental? We cannot be sure. Taken together, and with the different contexts of temple sacrifice and everyday normality, however, they do build up contrasting pictures, with Mary's scene feeling more domestic and comfortable.

At the heart of both stories is the promise of a baby. This is what dominates and resonates; this is the intentional centre for both stories. Yet again, there are many contrasts between the stories, too many for us to detail. Clearly, Mary's question is to be read as a request for clarification rather than an expression of doubt and disputation, but most significant is her humble acceptance: 'I am the Lord's servant' (v. 38, NIV). This is the response that would have been most appropriate for Zechariah, a righteous priest!

4 Songs of praise

Luke 1:39–56

One element in the contrasting stories of Zechariah and Mary might appear incidental but should not be overlooked. At the end of his encounter with Gabriel, Zechariah 'went to his home. After those days his wife Elizabeth conceived…' (1:23–24). After Mary's encounter, she 'got ready and hurried to a town in the hill country of Judea' (v. 39, NIV). Both sons will be special; both conceptions involve miraculous interventions by God, but, whereas John's conception involves a human father, Luke seems to be making it quite clear that Jesus' did not. Mary removes herself from the possibility of conceiving a child as the result of a sexual encounter with Joseph. This perspective is emphasised by the Spirit-inspired double blessing by Elizabeth on Mary (vv. 42, 45).

Within the narrative of the story, it is this blessing that releases the outpouring of praise from Mary towards God. Although the divine conception is properly a deep mystery, it is possible that Luke envisaged the conception as taking place in this moment of intimate praise. Elizabeth's words focus not only on Mary's belief but also on God's accomplishment: 'that there would be a fulfilment of what was spoken to her by the Lord' (v. 45). These dramatic moments between Elizabeth and Mary are resplendent (we could even say, 'pregnant') with the Spirit's presence. Mary's 'My soul magnifies the Lord' captures the sense of total response to God, and her words *from now on… for the Mighty One has done great things for me'* take on an even more focused and intense meaning.

Luke adds the comment, 'Mary remained with her for about three months' (v. 56). This might be a purely factual observation, but it does ensure that we know two things. First, the conception could not have been due to sexual activity with Joseph; Mary was away from Nazareth for the whole of this time. Second, Mary and Elizabeth would have been totally sure that she was pregnant, as she would have missed at least two periods. It may also reinforce the sense that the conception happened, in Luke's understanding, as Mary and Elizabeth met.

5 Christmas Day, full of angels

Luke 2:1–20

In verses 1–7, the birth of Jesus is described in the most matter-of-fact kind of way. It is set in a specific historic context and Joseph acts like everyone else around him: 'Joseph also went…' (v. 4). Then, in verse 9, the whole tone changes. Whereas verses 1–7 are political and prosaic, verses 9–20 are full of divine and dynamic responses. Verse 8 is pivotal, setting the scene for the celebration of Christ's birth.

The divine dimension to this birth is initiated by the arrival of the angel who 'stood before them' (v. 9). This is different language from that used to describe the appearance of the angel to either Zechariah or Mary. A more significant difference, however, is that 'the glory of the Lord shone around them'. This heightens the intensity of the visitation; it is striking that such language was absent even from the account of Zechariah in the temple, about to offer sacrifice near the altar.

The angel does not name himself but does deliver a message of 'good news'. Like some of the secular uses of this phrase, it refers to a birth—not the birth of an ordinary child or even a mere emperor, but 'a Saviour, who is the Messiah, the Lord' (v. 11). Each title has weighty significance. God promised to come and save his people; the Messiah was the anointed one of God, signalling the arrival of the new age; 'the Lord' was both Caesar's title and God's. Both the content and the context emphasise the in-breaking of God's presence.

The human responses are also noteworthy. Almost inevitably, the shepherds' response to the angel is terror (v. 9), yet they seem to observe and hear very clearly what has happened and what has been said (v. 15). They express no doubt, unlike Zechariah; rather, they act appropriately and 'with haste', like Mary (v. 16; 1:39). The appropriate response to a divine message spreads out ('all who heard it were amazed', v. 18), even though these messengers are ordinary mortals. Mary treasures and ponders the words, while the impact of the divine encounter on the shepherds continues as they return, 'glorifying and praising God' (v. 20).

As we participate in this account, we are immersed in the divine presence and the messages, and we are stimulated to respond empathetically with the characters. Perhaps this is one reason why today's reading is so highly treasured by us all.

6 The anticipation grows

Luke 2:21–40

Luke is concerned to emphasise in every possible way the veracity of his account, not only as historically viable but also as divinely authenticated. In this sense, it is witness rather than historiography. Luke knows that the divine dimension of the Christian claims for Jesus cannot be established directly by the historians' normal methods—but they can be established.

Chapter 2:1–20 establishes these claims though the appearance, message and praise of the angels, underlined by the 'glory of the Lord'— the manifest presence of God (see 9:30–31). Now Luke continues the process of authentication. The integrity of both Simeon and Anna is made clear. They are not people with vested interests; they are not naive shepherds but nor are they part of the religious hierarchy. They are thoroughly Jewish: for instance, Simeon is 'looking forward to the consolation of Israel' (v. 25). His testimony is that the promise given to him by the Holy Spirit has now been fulfilled; the Messiah has arrived. Not only does the Spirit rest on him permanently but the Spirit guides him to be in the right place at the right time to see the family as they come to the temple for purification. In this context of Jewish observance he recognises the reality of Jesus as Messiah—and more, for the baby will be 'a light for revelation to the Gentiles' too (v. 32).

Equally, the Jewish integrity of Anna is emphasised in many ways. Although the Holy Spirit is not mentioned and the whole narrative is much terser than in the account of Simeon, the impact is even more striking (v. 38). Her appearance is 'at that moment' (whether this means the moment of Mary's purification or of Simeon's prophecy is not specified); 'she came'—joining the party of witnesses; in response to the divine presence she 'began to praise God' (an expression of praise that is not part of her normal routine of worship) and she spoke about the child. We would probably love to know what she said, but the implication is that she announces the arrival of the one who will redeem Jerusalem— not the nations or the Gentiles, but Jerusalem.

Thus, at the heart of the Jewish nation, in the temple, in Jerusalem, there is a divinely appointed authentication of the significance of this child.

Guidelines

Reflect on the differences in the attitudes of Zechariah and Mary to Gabriel's words. How obvious are they? Do you feel that Gabriel's strikingly different responses are justified? Does this say anything to you about your own commitments and responses to God?

How important are angels in these stories, in the Bible more widely and in the theology and life of our churches? What are the roles of angels in the Bible? (Use a concordance to find more examples.) What might be the dangers in developing too much interest in angels? Conversely, what might we lose if we do not keep any awareness of them in our lives?

Re-read the various songs in these two chapters of Luke's Gospel—Elizabeth's, Mary's, Zechariah's, the angels' and Simeon's. What impact do these songs have on your emotions and your mind? Now, focusing on the birth of Jesus, express your own song of praise to God.

Incarnation (Part 2)

We continue our exploration of the significance of the incarnation, focusing on what it means to say that Jesus is fully human.

28 December–3 January

1 Jesus was tempted

Matthew 4:1–11

In this second week, we are going to concentrate on the true humanity of Jesus. An early bishop and theologian, St Gregory of Nazianzus, once said of Jesus, 'What he did not take on, he could not save.' He was arguing against someone who taught a partial incarnation, with bits of our humanity unvisited by Jesus. Gregory's great point was that only if Jesus shared every human faculty and experience could he help us.

In Matthew 4 we read the very familiar story of the temptations of Jesus. The crucial point for us, thinking about incarnation, is that these temptations—and the hunger that followed his fast (v. 2)—were completely real. Jesus was not playing a game; the temptations were deadly serious. Here, at the start of his public ministry, he was asked how he would carry it through. Would he use his power to avoid personal discomfort? Would he force his Father to do something spectacular and public, and so make everyone believe in him? Would he accept the throne of the world, which is his by right, the easy way—the way that did not lead through suffering? Each question was a real one, a genuine decision for him to make.

Could he have failed? Yes. If he is truly human, he could have failed. He could have made the wrong choice; he could have given in to temptation. This is always a possibility for a human being, and Jesus is a human being—God in the flesh, yes, but genuinely a human being.

We need to be careful about the nature of that 'could', however. Knowing the love of his Father and the power of the Spirit, and being determined himself to bring salvation to the world, it is inconceivable that he would have chosen the wrong path. Each choice was a real possibility for him, but he knew the nature of his mission too well, and was too committed to carrying it through, ever to give in to temptation. He was prevented from failing, though, by his human determination to do what he had come to do, not by some sort of divine shield—and so the writer to the Hebrews can encourage us to resist temptation in the same way Jesus did, because Jesus had no advantage over us (Hebrews 4:14–16).

2 Jesus' limited knowledge

Matthew 23:29–39

To be human is to be limited in many, many ways. Today we look at the limits of Jesus' knowledge. Although Jesus had greater than usual knowledge and insight, there were certainly things that he did not know: famously, when speaking about the coming of the day of judgement, he said, 'About that day or hour no one knows, neither the angels in heaven, nor the Son, but only the Father' (Mark 13:32). The passage we read today, however, suggests something more.

Matthew 23:29–39 comes at the end of a lengthy speech in which Jesus denounces the scribes and Pharisees for their hypocrisy, linking these religious leaders to those who, in earlier ages, killed God's prophets. Jerusalem, the city of David, the site of God's temple, was also the city that repeatedly killed God's prophets, and Jesus recalls that history to condemn its present religious leaders.

Jesus announces that they will be guilty of all innocent blood that has ever been shed, 'from the blood of righteous Abel to the blood of Zechariah son of Berechiah' (v. 35). This is odd, though; Zechariah son of Berechiah was the Old Testament prophet Zechariah (Zechariah 1:1), but we find no suggestion elsewhere that he died a violent death. A Zechariah who did was the son of Jehoiada, and his story is told in 2 Chronicles 24:20–22. He was killed by King Joash, despite his father's service to the king. Significantly, this Zechariah is the last prophet to be murdered in the historical books of the Old Testament—the last to be murdered in the Hebrew Bible in its standard arrangement.

It would make sense for Jesus to link this Zechariah to Abel—the last and the first servants of God to be killed in the Bible he knew. If this is right, however, Jesus got the name of the father wrong, thus suggesting a different Zechariah. It's an easy mistake to make.

We might want to insist that Jesus didn't make such mistakes. He was perfect, and perfection means not being subject to simple slips of memory. We might, however, suggest that the occasional lapse of memory is normal to humanity—not a moral failure, not a sin, but just a part of what it means to be limited in this world. If Jesus misremembers a surname, that is a demonstration that he is truly human, just as human as you and me.

3 Jesus prays

Matthew 26:31–46

To be human is to pray. We might make this claim on the basis of sociology: human beings are inveterate pray-ers, even those of us who say we do not believe in God. However, we are looking at the distinction and union between the divine and the human in Jesus: to be divine is to receive prayer, and to be human is to offer prayer.

In our passage today we see Jesus facing up to the fact that his suffering and death are imminent, and praying to the Father that somehow he might be able to avoid going through with it. He is praying that there might be another way. Prayer is the most intensely personal of all human activities but it is also a corporate activity, so he asks his friends, the disciples, to pray with him and for him, even as he withdraws from them so that his prayer might be appropriately private. Their repeated failure emphasises the loneliness of his calling: he has to face all the terrors of death, and all the weight of sin, utterly alone.

He prays to the Father, asking that there might be another way. His first prayer ends, 'Yet not what I want but what you want' (v. 39, NRSV). His second ends, 'If this cannot pass unless I drink it, your will be done' (v. 42, NRSV). The world does not change as he prays: still, the betrayer is leading the mob to arrest him; still, the leaders are planning to kill him; still, his disciples are weak and weary. The world does not change, but he does. His second prayer is more resolute than the first; the actions that follow are more resolute still. In prayer he finds the strength and courage to do what must be done.

To be human is to pray. Here we see Jesus at his most human, bent before the Father, begging that something might change, and discovering that the only thing that changes is himself. This is true prayer and true humanity. Jesus our brother prays as we have prayed, and as we long to pray. He is changed by his prayer, as we will be by ours.

4 Jesus heals

John 9:1–17

The ministry of Jesus is full of miracles. Healing miracles and exorcisms are particularly common. When we think about incarnation we might suppose that the miracles are signs of divine power—but there is another way of thinking about them.

In our reading today, we find Jesus healing a man born blind. The religious leaders are perturbed by this, because they have already decided that Jesus is a sinner from his attitude to sabbath laws. God does not and cannot work through a sinner, they reason, so God cannot be at work in Jesus' ministry. The man who has been healed is adamant, however: Jesus healed him; healing is God's work; therefore Jesus must be from God—that is, a prophet (v. 17).

Healing is indeed God's work, whether it happens through prayer and miracle or through careful medical attention. The nurse and the surgeon do the work of God just as much as the one who prays for healing. (I talked once to the medical director of a mission agency; he reflected that he had heard many testimonies of miraculous healing, but they tended to come from people who worked far from hospitals and medical care. Missionaries in cities tended to find their health restored through medical attention.) However healing comes, it is God's gift.

We might ask, though, did Jesus' ministry of healing come from his being God incarnate, or is it something that any human person empowered by the Spirit might do? Jesus is, after all, both God incarnate and a human being who is filled with the Spirit. If he performs miracles through his deity, they must be unique; if he performs miracles through his Spirit-empowered humanity, then we might expect, as human people empowered by the Spirit, to do similar things.

We can answer the question either way. Those of us who are committed to charismatic or Pentecostal traditions can find encouragement here; those of us who are suspicious of such traditions can answer the question the other way around. However, perhaps we should all reflect on what God can do through a person filled by the Spirit and raise our expectations and sights—for our own lives, and for the lives of our churches.

5 Jesus is resurrected

John 20:19–29

Jesus is truly human, the model for our humanity, and this remains true after death. Here, we read about one of the resurrection appearances of Jesus, and we learn something of the nature of the resurrection body. Jesus is still physical, corporeal: Thomas can touch him and feel him and recognise the continuity between this body and the one that died. At the same time, Jesus' presence is not impeded by locked doors (v. 19) or, it seems, by physical distance. The physical body that is his after the resurrection is more able than the physical body that was his before the resurrection—and we may assume that the physical body that will be ours after the resurrection will be similarly more able.

I was once asked to sign a doctrinal statement that contained the lines 'Jesus is truly God, of one substance with the Father, and was truly human, of one substance with us.' I refused, of course: the past tense is just wrong. Jesus is still, now, truly human, and always will be. Risen from the dead, he is truly human. Seated at the right hand of the Father, he is truly human. Coming again in glory, to judge the living and the dead, he will be truly human. To say 'Jesus was truly human' is a crass (although, in the context, I am sure, unintended) theological error.

The transformation of Jesus' humanity in his resurrection points to the transformation of our humanity in our coming resurrection. We will be changed. We will still be ourselves, defined by our stories and relationships, but the possibilities of our lives will be different. Knowing that Jesus is and always will be truly human, however, helps us to understand that this is what it means for us to be human; it is not something strange or transformative.

To believe in God's act in Jesus without having to see it—and to trust that this human story is God's own story and is therefore definitive, transformative, of every other human story—is an act of faith. 'Blessed,' says Jesus, 'are those who have not seen and yet have come to believe' (v. 29, NRSV).

6 Jesus stands with us in suffering

Revelation 1:9–20

The background to the book of Revelation is persecution. John is in exile because of his faith in Jesus, and he is writing to seven churches who all, in different ways, know what it is to be persecuted by the governing authorities because of their faith in Jesus. Chapter 1 gives us this wonderful image of Jesus (vv. 13–16): the details of his appearance are all drawn from Old Testament texts, linking Jesus once again with the messianic promises and the hope for the future of David's kingdom that we have seen.

Remarkably, however, John's first sight in the vision is not Jesus: it is seven lampstands (v. 12). The lampstands are explained at the end of the vision, along with another detail—the seven stars that Jesus holds in his right hand. The lampstands are the seven churches that John is writing to; the stars are the 'angels' of the churches (v. 20).

The first part of this explanation is easy enough, and powerful. John sees Jesus standing in the midst of the lampstands—that is, standing in the midst of the churches. The risen, exalted Jesus is not aloof from the struggles of his people, but is right there with them, standing in solidarity with them.

The stars are more difficult to interpret: 'the angels of the churches' might remind us of Byron's line, 'I wish he would explain his explanation!' Three different understandings have been proposed. The phrase might refer to guardian angels belonging to each individual church; it might refer to the inner spirit, the ethos, of each local church; or, if we note that 'angel' just means 'messenger', it might refer to those who speak God's word to the church, its leaders and teachers.

Whichever way we understand it, the vision is powerful: the churches, or their representatives, are held in Jesus' right hand. These are small and struggling churches (in chapters 2 and 3 we read letters from Jesus denouncing their many failures), but, for all this, Jesus stands with them and Jesus holds them fast. He, the incarnate one, knows our struggles and suffering, and he stands with us and holds us in the midst of it all.

Guidelines

In 1995 Joan Osborne had a hit with a song titled 'One of us'. The lyrics asked, 'What if God was one of us? Just a slob like one of us? Just a stranger on a bus?' The beating heart of Christian faith is the belief that, yes, God was and is one of us—that in the Jewish man Jesus of Nazareth, we look God full in the face, take God by the hand and have God sit down in our house or boat or town.

If others are offended by this claim, we should not be surprised. It is an inveterate human habit to imagine the divine as being simply separated from this world. Nor should we retreat from the endless implications of this claim on our own lives and thoughts and understandings. Our claim is that God has a face that some people, if not ourselves, have seen; that God spoke with a northern accent in Palestine; that God kissed a leper, and ignored his family, and debated with women, and dismissed demons. God was disturbingly present and local and active in that time and place.

Incarnation is an offensive idea, but it is a central Christian idea. God is happy to embrace a segment of our human history as his own story, and we are called to believe in response that every segment of our human history is embraced by God. As we saw in our final reading, God stands, in Jesus, in the midst of broken and failing and damaged churches. God holds those churches and their leaders in his right hand.

To believe in incarnation is, finally, to take our local church seriously. Such links, from the cosmic to the local, are the heart of what incarnation is about.

Supporting Barnabas in Schools with a gift in your will

Barnabas in Schools

For many charities, income from legacies is crucial in enabling them to plan ahead, and often provides the funding to develop new projects. Legacies make a significant difference to the ability of charities to achieve their purpose. In just this way, a legacy to support BRF's work would make a huge difference.

Take our Barnabas in Schools ministry, for example. In our increasingly secular society, fewer and fewer children are growing up with any real knowledge or understanding of the Bible or the Christian faith. We're passionate about enabling children and their teachers in primary schools to explore Christianity and the Bible creatively.

Our Barnabas RE Days, using storytelling, mime and drama, are in great demand. They explore big themes (such as 'What price peace?' looking at World War I and 'Why Narnia?' exploring 'The Chronicles of Narnia' in relation to Christianity), along with the major Christian festivals. We also offer specialist In-Service Training (INSET) sessions for teachers, along with a wide range of print and online resources. We are working with over 45,000 children each year through our schools work. In addition, we are actively contributing to the national debate about the value and place of RE in our schools and championing the vital importance of seeing RE (in particular, the teaching of Christianity) taken seriously in primary schools.

Throughout its history, BRF's ministry has been enabled thanks to the generosity of those who have shared its vision and supported its work, both by giving during their lifetime and also through legacy gifts.

A legacy gift would help fund the development and sustainability of BRF's Barnabas in Schools programme into the future. We hope you may consider a legacy gift to help us continue to take this work forward in the decades to come.

For further information about making a gift to BRF in your will or to discuss how a specific bequest could be used to develop our ministry, please contact Sophie Aldred (Head of Fundraising) or Richard Fisher (Chief Executive) by email at fundraising@brf.org.uk or by phone on 01865 319700.

The BRF
Magazine

The Gift of Years

Debbie Thrower

'Journey' is a deeply meaningful concept, especially when we think about growing older. BRF exists to resource your spiritual journey, and The Gift of Years is 'resourcing the spiritual journey of older people' in particular. Championing the fact that older people matter, we are celebrating the contribution that people make in their later years and resourcing ministry among this age group to help more people make the most of the gifts that come with increased longevity.

At the same time, there are huge challenges facing our rapidly ageing population. There is no underestimating the difficulties that longer life expectancy brings. Having a spiritual perspective on life can ease the path for those negotiating a way through longer life and inevitable physical decline, which is why the concept of 'journey' is such a significant one.

Christians believe that we all come from, and are journeying home to, the God who remembers us—literally 're-members' us. Memories of what has happened to us on our own journeys are selective. They contribute to our sense of identity. One of the tasks of old age is to sift our memories. Aberdeen University's Professor of Practical Theology, John Swinton, has said, 'Without the ability to forget, our memories cease to be uniquely important... Human memory is inevitably flawed, and open to deception and distortion. This, combined with our inherent fallenness, means that there is a real sense in which we can never know who we really are.' But, he adds, 'God is not uncertain about who we are.'

The premise that we are made in the image of God and are 'the apple of his eye' (Psalm 17:8) at *every* stage of our life underpins a Christian view of ageing. References to old age and its blessings appear throughout the Bible. Some of its greatest heroes were serving God's purposes well into old age—Abraham, Sarah, Moses and Anna, to name but a few.

A form of chaplaincy named after Anna lies at the heart of The Gift of Years. Anna appears, with Simeon, in Luke's Gospel. At the age of 84 she seized the opportunity to speak of redemption and is a fine role model of a faithful older person steeped in prayer.

Anna Chaplaincy is ecumenical, community-based and open to men and women, lay or ordained. Just as Messy Church began in a church in

Hampshire, so Anna Chaplaincy has grown out of pioneering ministry in another Hampshire town, Alton. More people are exploring this way of drawing alongside older people, helping individuals to negotiate the choppy waters of growing older in the 21st century.

Why is the journey tougher today than it might have been for previous generations? Medical advances make it possible for more of us to live longer, but the debate rages over the quality of life that such benefits afford. Families are more fragmented, many adults no longer living close to parents and grandparents. Relatives might even live on different continents and keep in touch by phone or computer. Society places a greater emphasis on being youthful, beautiful and productive. When older people are no longer economically active and health concerns loom large for them, they can be left fearful of 'becoming a burden'.

The message that older people matter is deeply countercultural. Churches dare not overlook the spiritual (as well as practical) needs of men and women in their later years—the widows, widowers those who are frail and dying—for younger generations are looking at the future, wondering whether the business of getting old is worth the candle.

Time spent as an Anna Chaplain convinces me of the necessity to hear the voices of older people, to share their wisdom and to see good role models of people living faithful lives, trusting in the God who made them and has cared for them along the way. It is a Christian duty to break the cycle of the fear of ageing and instil confidence instead.

While I was co-leading a course on 'Living Deeply and Well in Later Life', a day of sunshine and showers resulted in a spectacular rainbow above Lee Abbey in Devon. Many rushed outside to photograph it. One gentleman limped out rather more slowly to take in the view. He came and stood beside me, saying, 'I've come this week because my knees aren't working so well nowadays, and I need to draw more on my inner resources. Thank you for all that you're giving us.'

Such people show that wisdom comes in many guises, and some are older man- and woman-shaped! Paul said, 'We have this treasure in clay jars' (2 Corinthians 4:7). Yes, we are fragile, mortal vessels, but what an adventure it is to regard life as a journey of faith! The sixth-century Christian philosopher Boethius put it beautifully:

To see Thee is the end and the beginning;
Thou carriest me and thou goest before:
Thou art the journey and the journey's end.

Debbie Thrower is Team Leader of The Gift of Years (www.thegiftofyears.org
.uk). The Gift of Years: Bible reflections for older people is now available:
see page 155 to order.

An extract from
Peter's Preaching

As the earliest of the Gospels, Mark is arguably the foundational text of Christianity, summarising the core of Jesus' teaching. Vivid, immediate and provocative, it is in essence the preaching of Peter, Jesus' closest disciple, calling men and women to a more radical discipleship. In his new book, *Peter's Preaching*, Jeremy Duff brings to life the content and meaning of Mark's Gospel for contemporary readers, combining the in-depth analysis of a commentary with the accessibility of Bible reading notes. Each chapter explores a key theme from Mark; the following extract is from Chapter 9, 'The death of Jesus', commenting on Mark 15:1–37.

Within the richness and horror of this passage, I would draw attention to three points. First, we ought to take in the repulsive, horrendous suffering—the casual mention of flogging (v. 15), sufficient on its own to kill; the piercing with thorns (v. 17); the mockery (vv. 18–19, 29–32) and finally the long, slow, agonising suffocation of crucifixion itself (v. 24). We have perhaps grown so used to the idea of 'the crucifixion' that we forget what it actually involved, and we use words like 'sacrifice' glibly. Furthermore, a standard human reaction is to 'look away' from horror and pain, but if our calling is to follow Jesus, surely we must follow him, at least in our mind's eye, all the way to the cross. Paul later wrote:

I want to know Christ and the power of his resurrection and the sharing in his sufferings, becoming like him in his death, so that somehow I might achieve the resurrection from the dead.
PHILIPPIANS 3:10–11

We share in his sufferings so that we may also share in his glory.
ROMANS 8:17

Second, we can notice the theological irony in the passage. Jesus is proclaimed 'King of the Jews' by both the Romans and the temple authorities (vv. 18, 26, 32). They all think that the title is laughably ironic, since how could a dying man be king? Perhaps we might think the same—that Jesus can only be king when the shame of the cross has been wiped away by resurrection. Similarly, the idea that Jesus could be the Messiah, that he would destroy the temple and save others, is thrown back at him. These ideas were in the air and provided the context for his arrest, trial and condemnation; but again it is assumed that his death must prove these claims false. It is a picture of the finality of death, making a mockery of hopes and dreams.

However, we should remember Jesus' discussion with James and John (Mark 10:35–40). They asked 'to sit, one on your right-hand and one on your left in your glory', to which Jesus replied, 'To sit at my right and my left is not for me to grant—it is for those for whom it has been prepared.' I believe that this connection is the reason why Peter bothered to provide the detail that one bandit was crucified on Jesus' left and one on the right. If so, then the crucifixion is not a tragedy and a shameful event; it is Jesus' glory. This interpretation is certainly developed in John's Gospel, where the idea of Jesus being 'glorified' seems to be connected with his death (for example, 12:23; 13:31), and in Revelation, where Jesus is given glory because of his death (5:9–12). His death, far from proving that he is not the Messiah, actually proves that he is, for, as he said numerous times, his death was necessary and he was prepared to go through it.

> *We see Jesus experiencing the horror of feeling utterly alone and forsaken*

Third, there is the darkness—physical (v. 33) and, more importantly, spiritual darkness (v. 34) as Jesus cries out that he has been forsaken. There have been some attempts to claim that, since this is the first line from Psalm 22, Jesus really had in mind the hopeful way in which the psalm ends. But if that was the meaning that Peter wanted to give us, why did he not quote the ending? No, if we read the text straightforwardly, we see Jesus experiencing the horror of feeling utterly alone and forsaken, even by the God he called 'father', whose will he accepted (14:36). Gone is the confidence of the passion predictions, as the true horror of a pain-filled, torturous death is faced.

Many people, understandably and even rightly, are frustrated or angry with God because he doesn't seem to answer their prayers in times of suffering. Here we see what has been called 'the most unanswered prayer in history'. God did not answer Jesus' cry of pain and frustration as he hung dying. Jesus knew the agony of feeling that God had turned his face away from him. The rest of the story demonstrates that God had not actually abandoned him at all, but at the time, even Jesus could not hold on to that truth.

> *Jesus' death is seen as the place of revelation, of judgement and of victory*

How can we respond? First, we can express thankfulness and awe at the depth of love that was willing to endure even this agony to welcome us back to God. We should remember that Jesus had known and told his disciples, weeks before, what would happen when he reached Jerusalem. However, we are also reminded of the terrible pressure brought by insult and apparent failure. We see it often enough in the media; maybe we know people going through similar experiences; maybe we have endured it ourselves. There is no answer, but there is one consolation—that in such experiences we model Christ.

Done

Jesus' final words in John's Gospel are 'It is finished'—words which bring together both the cry of the broken, tortured body entering the release of death and the cry of victory as God's saving work is achieved. These words are not expressed in Peter's preaching, but the same sentiment is there.

Jesus gave a loud cry and died. The curtain of the temple was torn in two from top to bottom. When the centurion who stood facing him saw how he died, he said, 'Truly this man was the Son of God.'
MARK 15:37–39

We have already considered this passage because this is the first time that a human recognises Jesus as 'Son of God'. We have also noted the divine judgement against the temple (represented by the torn curtain), whose authorities had rejected Jesus and arranged his death. Nevertheless, we cannot end a study of Jesus' death without revisiting Mark's words here.

Jesus' death—not his resurrection—is seen as the place of revelation, of judgement and of victory. Again we must say, if you want to see what Jesus is really like and what 'Son of God' really means, look at the man dying on the cross.

A strong, consistent message is coming through from our study. Jesus' faced his death willingly. He knew what was coming; he could have escaped it easily, but he didn't. His death was 'for many': it was a ransom, a sacrifice. It was God's great act of saving power, it brought about the new covenant and it brought about God's reign.

Jesus' death in Peter's preaching can be summed up that easily. However, its implications are so enormous, so central to Christian theology, spirituality and mission, that a further book could be written unpacking them. For now, though, let us consider three final reflections. Dare we follow Jesus' and John the Baptist's example in challenging power, despite its potential cost to us? Can we grasp the fact that Jesus' sacrifice was for many, not for a few? Can we hold on to the assurance that Jesus has experienced the pain of insult, abandonment and apparent failure himself, but that it was not the end of the story?

The Revd Dr Jeremy Duff has taught New Testament at Oxford University and a number of theological colleges and courses, and is a vicar in an urban parish in the Diocese of Liverpool. For ten years he was one of the commissioning editors for Guidelines *and his book* The Elements of New Testament Greek (2005) *is Cambridge University Press's bestselling religion title.*

To order a copy of Peter's Preaching, *please turn to the order form on page 155.*

An extract from
Comings and Goings

Comings and **Goings**

Retracing the Christmas story through place and time

Gordon Giles

In BRF's 2015 Advent book, Gordon Giles invites us on a journey from the end of time to the beginning. Working backwards from the Advent 'Four Last Things'—death, judgement, heaven and hell—we travel via Jesus' life, death and resurrection to the events of Christmas and, finally, to the dawn of creation. En route, we visit some of the Holy Land sites associated with Gospel events. This extract is entitled 'Holding the light: Simeon and Anna', based on Luke 2:22–32, 36–38.

It is usually possible for tourists and pilgrims to visit Temple Mount (Haram al-Sharif) in Jerusalem. Muslims should go up there, Jews must not and Christians may do so, for on a raised area above the former Western Wall of the temple is situated the al-Aqsa Mosque and the Dome of the Rock. The first king of Jordan, Abdullah I, was murdered there and his tomb is nearby. The Dome of the Rock is revered by Muslims as the place from which the prophet Mohammed ascended into heaven, and also by Jews, Christians and Muslims as the place where Isaac was so nearly sacrificed by Abraham (Genesis 22:1–18). Jews may not go up there because, since the temple was destroyed by the Romans after the uprising in AD70, no one can be sure exactly where the Holy of Holies was, and it is not acceptable to trangress its sacred boundaries accidentally. Only priests such as Zechariah were allowed to enter it, and then only once in their lifetime.

For Christians, it is an eerie yet beautiful place of tranquillity above the hustle and bustle of modern Jerusalem. Despite the security checks, stacked-up riot shields and machine gun-toting guards who nonchalantly stroll around, one can hope for a peaceful visit while being struck by the proximity of violence and danger. When Ariel Sharon visited the site on 28 September 2000, the Palestinians were furious and a major uprising was ignited. Sharon was elected Israeli Prime Minister within six months. He died in 2014.

The temple complex was the holiest site in Judaism, and it was customary for a firstborn male child to be taken to the temple to be redeemed (bought back) from the Lord. The custom derived from the aftermath of the Israelites' flight from Egypt under Moses: in Exodus 13:2 and 11–16 the people are told to dedicate their firstborn sons to God. There was also a sseparate tradition of the purification of the mother, 40 days after a male birth or 80 days after a female birth (Leviticus 12:6–8). It is with this rite of purification that the sacrificial turtle doves are associated: parents were expected to offer a ram and a pigeon, or, if they could not afford a ram, two doves.

Because a mother would not be able to visit the temple within the first 40 days, the two rites were often combined, such that the story in Luke can be a little confusing: Jesus is redeemed and his mother is purified at the same time. We know from the story that Mary and Joseph were devout but poor parents, keen to do the right thing by God and by their unusually conceived firstborn son. Nowadays we commemorate this event in the church year as the final day of the 40-day Christmas season—2 February, also known as Candlemas. Simeon was the first to recognise Jesus as the 'light of the Gentiles'—the saviour of all nations, not only the Jews. It is a crucial event, and is prophetic in its scope as the aged Simeon and Anna recognise and reveal who Jesus is.

There is another, fundamentally human dimension to this story, which any grandparent will recognise. Simeon and Anna were not Jesus' grandparents, of course—they were perhaps more like his god-parents—but, as each of them holds the 40-day old Christ in their arms, there are resonances for anyone who holds a baby for the first time. There is something wonderfully profound, something inherently hopeful, as one generation embraces another. In their hopeful embrace of Christly youth, Simeon and Anna show us what we should hope for and embrace. They teach us to relish the salvation we have now seen through their eyes. Whatever age we are, whether we have recently turned 20, 40, 50, 60, 70 or 80, we, like Simeon and Anna, have seen the salvation that has been prepared for us in the birth, death and resurrection of Jesus Christ.

But borne upon the throne
Of Mary's gentle breast,
Watched by her duteous love,
In her fond arms at rest;
Thus to his Father's house
He comes, the heavenly guest.

There Joseph at her side
In reverent wonder stands;
And, filled with holy joy,
Old Simeon in his hands
Takes up the promised Child,
The glory of all lands.

JOHN ELLERTON (1826–93)

The Revd Dr Gordon Giles is Vicar of St Mary Magdalene's Church in Enfield, North London and has led many pilgrimages to the Holy Land.

Recommended reading

Kevin Ball

Who wrote Mark's Gospel? At first glance, this may seem a ridiculous question and not one you've thought much about. Mark's name isn't on the list of the twelve disciples, yet, remarkably, large chunks of his Gospel appear in both Matthew and Luke's Gospels, suggesting that his writing was highly respected from the earliest times of the church. So how did this come about?

Jeremy Duff provides insightful answers in his new book *Peter's Preaching: The message of Mark's Gospel*, revealing that an ancient source describes Mark as Peter's translator to a Greek-speaking world. Intriguingly, the same source tells us that, while Mark recorded Peter's stories of Jesus 'accurately', he did not record them 'in order'. Mark devised his own sequence for the stories, for his own purpose, using a structure and format as radical in the first century as ebooks are today.

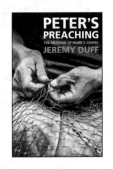

That is only the start of Jeremy's detective work in this stimulating book, which tries to uncover Peter's thought process on the key themes of the Christian message. Jeremy pieces them together like a jigsaw to reveal the full picture of Peter's understanding and explains and how that understanding helps us to grasp the radical nature of the Christian faith in those early years of the church.

So why didn't Mark present Peter's preaching in this same way? What was his purpose in presenting Peter's account 'out of order'? Jeremy turns his attention to this in the second part of the book, noting, as many previous commentators have done, that the key is the 'hinge' in the middle of the Gospel, with Peter's 'confession of faith' on the road to Caesarea Philippi and the transfiguration (Mark 8:27—9:8). Up to this point, Mark uses Peter's stories to explore the question 'Who is Jesus?' At the hinge point, Peter gives the right answer, 'You are the

Messiah', which serves only to open up a deeper question: what does that mean? The second part of the Gospel explores this question in the extended details of the events leading to the crucifixion.

The work done by Jeremy to uncover Peter's preaching illuminates Mark's purpose, which can only be found in understanding Jesus' radical way of approaching life and relationships. Unlike so many leaders of our time, Jesus embodies his radical message: the message and the person cannot be separated. There are no inconsistencies shaped by a need to appeal to prevailing cultural moods; there is no hiding behind carefully selected statistics presented as soundbites; there is nothing to expose in a scandal. Mark's challenge to his readers was and always will be: 'From my stories, who do you think Jesus is and are you ready to embrace his countercultural revolution?

Peter's Preaching
The message of Mark's Gospel
Jeremy Duff
pb, 978 0 85746 350 0, £9.99. Also available for Kindle

What is contemplation? Perhaps this is another question that you have not often considered. Contemplation is an approach to spiritual living that has a very long history. It has helped many people to plumb the depths of prayer, through silence, to hear God's voice and discover a relationship with him not experienced previously.

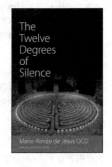

Much of the discussion on the theme from past centuries appears in the writings of the so-called Christian mystics, whose work was propelled by love and the desire for inner perfection. The mystics detail the course of this interior scrutiny and document their journey with imagery to help define the way. For instance, St Teresa of Avila used the rooms of a castle; St Clare of Assisi, a mirror; St Catherine of Siena, a bridge; and St Thérèse of Lisieux, a flower.

Nineteenth-century French Carmelite nun Sister Marie-Aimée de Jésus introduces another way, progressing by degrees to explore the channel to God that is provided through silence—a way that Carmelite writer Edith Stein has brought to wider attention. Sister Marie-Aimée's work is edited and translated into English by Lucinda M. Vardey in *The Twelve Degrees of Silence*.

Much of Marie-Aimée's spirituality and approach to exploring the interior self before God was influenced by the writings of St John of the Cross. What differentiates John's and Marie-Aimée's contributions, however, is that his work defines the rule, while hers provides directions. *The Twelve Degrees of Silence*, through probing questions for reflection, points to the stages a person needs to undergo to bring 'Jesus to life' within and to be transformed slowly to the place where 'there will be nothing left but Christ'.

There is no formal methodology for praying the twelve degrees, but the degrees themselves, by their very nature, fall into four specific groups.

- Marie-Aimée regards the first three degrees as preparation to becoming 'the silent servant of Divine Love'. They cover Silence in Words, Silence in Actions and Silence with One's Imagination.
- The next three open us up to hear 'the first note of the sacred song, the song of the heavens': Silence with One's Memories, Silence with Others and Silence with One's Heart.
- The following three are aids to perfecting a simple purity, considered as 'blessed childhood': Silence to Self-Interest, Silence of the Mind and Silence to Judgements.
- The last three prepare and experience the gift of silence as an eternal state of unity: Silence to the Will, Silence towards Oneself and Silence with God.

Whatever happens, the assurance that all will certainly be better than it was, that the rewards and treasures are indeed worth the toil, is what draws us to journey. (Sister Marie-Aimée de Jésus)

The Twelve Degrees of Silence
Marie-Aimée de Jésus OCD
pb, 978 0 85746 407 1, 80 pages, £6.99

You can look inside and find out more about all BRF books on our website: www.brfonline.org. You can also follow us on Twitter: @brfonline and like us on Facebook, www.facebook.com/biblereadingfellowship.

As a Christian charity, BRF is involved in seven complementary areas.

- **BRF** (www.brf.org.uk) resources adults for their spiritual journey through Bible reading notes, books and Quiet Days. BRF also provides the infrastructure that supports our other specialist ministries.
- **Messy Church** (www.messychurch.org.uk), led by Lucy Moore, enables churches all over the UK (and increasingly abroad) to reach children and adults beyond the fringes of the church.
- **Barnabas in Churches** (www.barnabasinchurches.org.uk) helps churches to support, resource and develop their children's ministry with the under-11s more effectively .
- **Barnabas in Schools** (www.barnabasinschools.org.uk) enables primary school children and teachers to explore Christianity creatively and bring the Bible alive within RE and Collective Worship.
- **Faith in Homes** (www.faithinhomes.org.uk) supports families to explore and live out the Christian faith at home.
- **Who Let The Dads Out** (www.wholetthedadsout.org) inspires churches to engage with dads and their pre-school children.
- **The Gift of Years** (www.brf.org.uk/thegiftofyears) celebrates the blessings of long life and seeks to meet the spiritual needs of older people.

At the heart of BRF's ministry is a desire to equip adults and children for Christian living—helping them to read and understand the Bible, explore prayer and grow as disciples of Jesus. We need your help to make an impact on the local church, local schools and the wider community.

- You could support BRF's ministry with a one-off gift or regular donation (using the response form on page 153).
- You could consider making a bequest to BRF in your will.
- You could encourage your church to support BRF as part of your church's giving to home mission—perhaps focusing on a specific area of our ministry, or a particular member of our Barnabas team.
- Most important of all, you could support BRF with your prayers.

If you would like to discuss how a specific gift or bequest could be used in the development of our ministry, please phone 01865 319700 or email enquiries@brf.org.uk.

Whatever you can do or give, we thank you for your support.

BRF has been helping individuals connect with the Bible for over 90 years. We want to support churches as they seek to encourage church members into regular Bible reading.

Order a Bible reading resources pack

This pack is designed to give your church the tools to publicise our Bible reading notes. It includes:

- Sample Bible reading notes for your congregation to try.
- Publicity resources, including a poster.
- A church magazine feature about Bible reading notes.

The pack is free, but we welcome a £5 donation to cover the cost of postage. If you require a pack to be sent outside the UK or require a specific number of sample Bible reading notes, please contact us for postage costs. More information about what the current pack contains is available on our website.

How to order and find out more

- Visit www.biblereadingnotes.org.uk/for-churches/
- Telephone BRF on 01865 319700 between 9.15 am and 5.30 pm.
- Write to us at BRF, 15 The Chambers, Vineyard, Abingdon, OX14 3FE

Keep informed about our latest initiatives

We are continuing to develop resources to help churches encourage people into regular Bible reading, wherever they are on their journey. Join our email list at **www.biblereadingnotes.org.uk/helpingchurches/** to stay informed about the latest initiatives that your church could benefit from.

Introduce a friend to our notes

We can send information about our notes and current prices for you to pass on. Please contact us.

BRF MINISTRY APPEAL RESPONSE FORM

I would like to help BRF. Please use my gift for:

❑ Where most needed ❑ Barnabas Children's Ministry ❑ Messy Church
❑ Who Let The Dads Out? ❑ The Gift of Years

Please complete all relevant sections of this form and print clearly.

Title _____ First name/initials _____ Surname _____
Address _____
_____ Postcode _____
Telephone _____ Email _____

Regular giving

If you would like to give by direct debit, please tick the box below and fill in details:

❑ I would like to make a regular gift of £ _____ per month / quarter / year
(delete as appropriate) by Direct Debit. (Please complete the form on page 159.)

If you would like to give by standing order, please contact Priscilla Kew (tel: 01235 462305; email priscilla.kew@brf.org.uk; write to BRF address below).

One-off donation

Please accept my special gift of
❑ £10 ❑ £50 ❑ £100 (other) £ _____ by

❑ Cheque / Charity Voucher payable to 'BRF'
❑ Visa / Mastercard / Charity Card
(delete as appropriate)

Name on card _____

Card no. ☐☐☐☐ ☐☐☐☐ ☐☐☐☐ ☐☐☐☐

Start date ☐☐☐   Expiry date ☐☐☐

Security code ☐☐☐

Signature _____ Date _____

❑ I would like to give a legacy to BRF. Please send me further information.

❑ I want BRF to claim back tax on this gift.
(If you tick this box, please fill in gift aid declaration overleaf.)

Please detach and send this completed form to: BRF, 15 The Chambers, Vineyard, Abingdon OX14 3FE.   BRF is a Registered Charity (No.233280)

GIFT AID DECLARATION

Bible Reading Fellowship

Please treat as Gift Aid donations all qualifying gifts of money made:

today ☐   in the past 4 years ☐   in the future ☐

I confirm I have paid or will pay an amount of Income Tax and/or Capital Gains Tax for each tax year (6 April to 5 April) that is at least equal to the amount of tax that all the charities that I donate to will reclaim on my gifts for that tax year. I understand that other taxes such as VAT or Council Tax do not qualify. I understand that BRF will reclaim 25p of tax on every £1 that I give.

☐   My donation does not qualify for Gift Aid.

Signature _____

Date _____

Notes:

1. Please notify BRF if you want to cancel this declaration, change your name or home address, or no longer pay sufficient tax on your income and/or capital gains.

2. If you pay Income Tax at the higher/additional rate and want to receive the additional tax relief due to you, you must include all your Gift Aid donations on your Self-Assessment tax return or ask HM Revenue and Customs to adjust your tax code.

BRF PUBLICATIONS ORDER FORM

Please send me the following book(s):

		Quantity	Price	Total
376 0	Comings and Goings (*G. Giles*)	_____	£7.99	_____
350 0	Peter's Preaching (*J. Duff*)	_____	£9.99	_____
407 1	The Twelve Degrees of Silence (*Marie-Aimée de Jésus*)	_____	£5.99	_____
424 8	The Word Was God (*A. John*)	_____	£6.99	_____
651 1	Mary (*A. Jones*)	_____	£8.99	_____
353 1	The Barnabas 365 Story Bible (*S.A. Wright*)	_____	£12.99	_____
178 0	My Keepsake Bible (*S.A. Wright*)	_____	£8.99	_____
412 5	The Barnabas Page-a-Day Bible (*R. Davies*)	_____	£10.99	_____
380 7	The Whoosh Bible (*G. Robins*)	_____	£12.99	_____
413 2	The Gift of Years (Bible reading notes)	_____	£2.50	_____

POSTAGE AND PACKING CHARGES				
Order value	UK	Europe	Economy (Surface)	Standard (Air)
Under £7.00	£1.25	£3.00	£3.50	£5.50
£7.00–£29.00	£2.25	£5.50	£6.50	£10.00
£30.00 & over	free	prices on request		

Total for books £ _____
Donation £ _____
Post & packing £ _____
TOTAL £ _____

Please complete the payment details below and send with payment to: **BRF, 15 The Chambers, Vineyard, Abingdon OX14 3FE**

Name _____

Address _____

_____ Postcode _____

Tel _____ Email _____

Total enclosed £ _____ (cheques should be made payable to 'BRF')

Please charge my Visa ❑ Mastercard ❑ Switch card ❑ with £ _____

Card no: ☐☐☐☐ ☐☐☐☐ ☐☐☐☐ ☐☐☐☐ ☐☐☐☐

Expires ☐☐☐☐   Security code ☐☐☐

Issue no (Switch only) ☐☐☐☐

Signature (essential if paying by credit/Switch) _____

GUIDELINES INDIVIDUAL SUBSCRIPTIONS

❑ I would like to take out a subscription myself:

Your name _____

Your address _____

_____ Postcode _____

Tel _____ Email _____

Please send *Guidelines* beginning with the January 2016 / May 2016 / September 2016 issue: (delete as applicable)

(please tick box)	UK	Europe/Economy	Standard
GUIDELINES	❑ £16.35	❑ £24.00	❑ £27.60
GUIDELINES 3-year sub	❑ £42.75		

Please complete the payment details below and send with appropriate payment to: **BRF, 15 The Chambers, Vineyard, Abingdon OX14 3FE**

Total enclosed £ _____ (cheques should be made payable to 'BRF')

Please charge my Visa ❑ Mastercard ❑ Switch card ❑ with £ _____

Card no: | | | | | | | | | | | | | | | | | | |

Expires | | | | | Security code | | | |

Issue no (Switch only) | | | | |

Signature (essential if paying by card) _____

To set up a direct debit, please also complete the form on page 159 and send it to BRF with this form.

BRF is a Registered Charity

GL0315

GUIDELINES GIFT SUBSCRIPTIONS

❏ I would like to give a gift subscription (please provide both names and addresses:

Your name _____

Your address _____

_____ Postcode _____

Tel _____ Email _____

Gift subscription name _____

Gift subscription address _____

_____ Postcode _____

Gift message (20 words max. or include your own gift card for the recipient)

_____

_____

Please send *Guidelines* beginning with the January 2016 / May 2016 / September 2016 issue: (delete as applicable)

(please tick box)	UK	Europe/Economy	Standard
GUIDELINES	❏ £16.35	❏ £24.00	❏ £27.60
GUIDELINES 3-year sub	❏ £42.75		

Please complete the payment details below and send with appropriate payment to: **BRF, 15 The Chambers, Vineyard, Abingdon OX14 3FE**

Total enclosed £ _____ (cheques should be made payable to 'BRF')

Please charge my Visa ❏ Mastercard ❏ Switch card ❏ with £ _____

Card no: ⬚⬚⬚⬚⬚⬚⬚⬚⬚⬚⬚⬚⬚⬚⬚⬚⬚⬚⬚

Expires ⬚⬚⬚⬚ Security code ⬚⬚⬚

Issue no (Switch only) ⬚⬚⬚⬚

Signature (essential if paying by card) _____

To set up a direct debit, please also complete the form on page 159 and send it to BRF with this form.

Now you can pay for your annual subscription to BRF notes using Direct Debit. You need only give your bank details once, and the payment is made automatically every year until you cancel it. If you would like to pay by Direct Debit, please use the form opposite, entering your BRF account number under 'Reference'.

You are fully covered by the Direct Debit Guarantee:

The Direct Debit Guarantee

- This Guarantee is offered by all banks and building societies that accept instructions to pay Direct Debits.
- If there are any changes to the amount, date or frequency of your Direct Debit, The Bible Reading Fellowship will notify you 10 working days in advance of your account being debited or as otherwise agreed. If you request The Bible Reading Fellowship to collect a payment, confirmation of the amount and date will be given to you at the time of the request.
- If an error is made in the payment of your Direct Debit, by The Bible Reading Fellowship or your bank or building society, you are entitled to a full and immediate refund of the amount paid from your bank or building society.
  - – If you receive a refund you are not entitled to, you must pay it back when The Bible Reading Fellowship asks you to.
- You can cancel a Direct Debit at any time by simply contacting your bank or building society. Written confirmation may be required. Please also notify us.

The Bible Reading Fellowship

Instruction to your bank or building society to pay by Direct Debit

Please fill in the whole form using a ballpoint pen and send to The Bible Reading Fellowship, 15 The Chambers, Vineyard, Abingdon OX14 3FE.

Service User Number: | 5 | 5 | 8 | 2 | 2 | 9 |

Name and full postal address of your bank or building society

To: The Manager	Bank/Building Society
Address	
	Postcode

Name(s) of account holder(s)

Branch sort code

| | | | | | |

Bank/Building Society account number

| | | | | | | | | |

Reference

| | | | | | | |

Instruction to your Bank/Building Society

Please pay The Bible Reading Fellowship Direct Debits from the account detailed in this instruction, subject to the safeguards assured by the Direct Debit Guarantee.
I understand that this instruction may remain with The Bible Reading Fellowship and, if so, details will be passed electronically to my bank/building society.

Signature(s)
Date

Banks and Building Societies may not accept Direct Debit instructions for some types of account.

This page is intentionally left blank.